HOW TO
SELL YOUR HOME
IN A
DOWN MARKET

The Facts:

- From New York to Florida, the Midwest, and California, real estate is down by 10 to 30 percent.

- Overbuilding has created more homes than there are people to buy them.

- The S&L crisis and government housing auctions will further reduce the value of your real estate investment.

The Solution:

Comprehensive, realistic, and authoritative, *How to Sell Your Home in a Down Market* is a "can-do" crash course in selling your home and preserving the most important investment of your life.

HOW TO
SELL YOUR HOME
IN A
DOWN MARKET

Robert Irwin

WARNER BOOKS

A Time Warner Company

Warner Books, Inc.
666 Fifth Avenue
New York, NY 10103

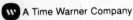 A Time Warner Company

First printing: May 1991

10 9 8 7 6 5 4 3 2 1

Cover design by Tom Tafuri/One Plus One Studio
Production services by BMR, Corte Madera, CA
   Copy edit: Jim Nageotte
   Index: Ann Goodyear
   Proofreader: Andrea Fox
   Text design: Steve Wozenski
   Page makeup: Steve Wozenski
   Project management: Jack E. Jennings

Library of Congress Cataloging-in-Publication Data
Irwin, Robert, 1941-
   How to sell your home in a down market / by Robert Irwin
      p.   cm.
   Includes index.
   ISBN 0-446-39298-7
   1. House selling.   2. Real estate business.   I. Title.
HD1379.I652 1991
333.33'83—dc20   91-6719
                                     CIP

Table of Contents

Introduction   i

1   Yes You Can!   1

2   What Your House is Worth Today   13

3   How to Get Good Exposure for Your Home   27

4   Auctions   47

5   Clean and Paint   61

6   Promotional Giveaways that Sell Homes   69

7   Saving on the Commission   85

8   Five Ways Out   99

9   When to Bail Out   125

10   How to Avoid Foreclosure   137

11   Tax Consequences of Foreclosure   163

12   Refinancing to Get Your Money Out   173

13   Watch Out for "Sales Exhaustion"   185

14   When the Next Upturn Comes   191

Index   193

Today's Real Estate Crash

JoAnn and David bought their home in California three years ago. At the time, prices were soaring, and David and JoAnn had to stretch their budget to the breaking point to get in. But, they were told, "If you don't buy now, you may never be able to own a California home!" And, "Housing prices in California only go up!"

They bought using an adjustable rate mortgage in which the payments could increase, depending on market conditions. They've increased ever since.

Recently, with the recession of the early 1990s, David was laid off work. JoAnn held onto her job, but one income wasn't enough to make those increasing monthly payments. So, sadly, they decided to sell. That's when they got the shock of their lives.

Not only had housing prices not gone up, they had turned around and gone down. Because JoAnn and David had bought at the peak of the market, their house was worth 25 percent less today than what they had paid for it. Since they had only put 20 percent down, that meant it was actually worth less than what the mortgage was!

JoAnn and David had some grim alternatives. They could sit in the house and continue trying to make the mortgage payments. Or they could try to sell for higher than the market price. Or they could walk away and lose everything.

When I last talked with them, they had the house up for sale above market, and they were trying to rent out some of their bedrooms to students from a nearby college in the hope of getting enough money to make the monthly payments. The trouble was they only had a three bedroom home, and students couldn't afford high rent. And they hadn't had any nibbles from buyers.

If JoAnn and David were an isolated case, it would be simple enough to feel sorry for them momentarily, and then go on with our lives. But they represent not an isolated case or even a tiny minority, but a large proportion of homeowners today, not just in California, but around the country. As I write this, most areas of the country are in a severe real estate recession (not to mention an economic downturn as well) with falling prices. Those who must sell are the hardest hit.

What Happened to Real Estate?

What happened to the old adage with regard to real estate, mentioned so often over the last few decades, that, "It's the only investment you'll ever make that always goes up in value"?

Actually, until recently it's been quite true. Since the end of World War II, real estate prices have consistently moved upward in most of the country. In some areas, such as California and Florida, there was a perpetual boom with a forty year price history averaging increases of at least 5 percent a year.

When it came time to buy a home, in fact, the argument was frequently used by real estate brokers that you shouldn't worry too much about price because there was no way you could lose. Yes, you could lose money in stocks, bonds, or commodities, but never in real estate. It was the one area where there were no price declines. This argument, in fact, was made to convince many home buyers to spend more than they felt was prudent on their homes. "Get in now before the price goes higher" was a frequently spoken slogan that got buyers to pay ever higher prices.

If you bought within the last few years, you well know the truth of what I'm saying. You now also know a different and unfortunate truth—it was a lie.

Today in the vast majority of the country prices are moving downward, not upward. According to a study from the University of California at Berkeley, real estate owners lost over $70 billion in property values during 1990 alone. If that's divided equally among the 51.8 million home owners in this country, it works out to roughly $1,351 per home.

Of course, in the real world the declines are not really averaged out over everybody. Some people lost less, others a whole lot more. In addition, this study was for one year only. Over the past three years the decline has probably averaged closer to $5,000 per owner!

Does that mean that your house has gone down $5,000 in value? Not if you live in that roughly 20 percent of the country where prices have been level or actually gone up, places like Sacramento, California and the greater Seattle, Washington area.

But if you live in the other 80 percent of the country, it's a different story. In southern California, for example, you've probably seen a loss of at least $25,000 on your home (more if your home was priced above $200,000).

In Texas your loss was probably closer to $50,000, if you go back to 1985. (As of this writing, the market in Texas is actually improving!)

In Kansas and Nebraska it may have been only $20,000 and most of that came in the early 1980s. But in the Boston area and upstate New York, it could be as high as $40,000 or more, depending again on the price range your home is in.

A New Down Side

In short, we have learned that like other investments, real estate, too, has its down side. But what exactly does that mean to you, individually, as a home owner?

If you plan not to sell but instead to stay in your home for a long time and not try to borrow against it, it probably means nothing. Your mortgage payments will remain the same (unless you have an adjustable rate mortgage) as will your other costs, although in some states you might get a little relief in terms of reduced property taxes. (Not so in most states where taxes are not raised or reduced except on sale.) In short, yesterday your house might have been worth $110,000. Today it's worth $90,000. But it's the same house with the same creaks in the floor, the same cracks in the ceiling, and the same address on the street. If you don't sell or borrow against it, nothing's changed.

On the other hand, if you try to *sell* your property, everything's changed. When you try to sell your house, you join the ranks of hundreds of thousands of others who are also trying to sell.

Selling in a Buyer's Market

Only today it's a buyers market. No longer can you expect to get an acceptable offer within a few weeks or even a few months. Many brokers are now telling their sellers they can expect to wait six months to a year before they even get an offer! And that offer, when it comes, might be for only a fraction of the asking price.

In short, if you want or need to sell your home right now, you've picked the worst time in the last fifty years to do it. Today buyers are gloating over the deals they can make, the choices they have. At the same time sellers are wringing their hands over the losses they have to take, the time they have to wait. Some sellers can't even sell their homes at any price! (One couple I know near Los Angeles has dropped their price $65,000 below market and still has not had one offer!)

Does any of this sound familiar?

What Can You Do?

The reason you picked up this book is that you are thinking about selling your house . . . and you're worried. You may have read stories in the newspapers about today's down market. Perhaps you've tried to sell and have experienced the problems first hand.

What should be clear to you is that today it's a different ball game. Selling today is not like it was only a year or two ago. Times are different, and new methods and techniques are called for. You will find them in this book.

This book will give you solutions. It will show you ways to avoid taking a huge loss. It will give you ideas on how to sell quickly without waiting six months to a year. In short, it will give you some positive answers, some real help in selling that house of yours.

Begin with a Positive Approach

The place to get started is in your own head. You can only sell your house if you have a positive approach. So let's get started with these positive thoughts:

You *can* sell your house in this market. (It's possible to sell any house in any market, if you use proven techniques.)

You *can* sell in a reasonable amount of time. (You just need to get the proper exposure and marketing.)

You *can* sell for more. (It's mostly a matter of getting the buyer to fall in love with the property, not the price.)

Selling in a down market requires rethinking both the methods you use to find buyers as well as what your real equity in your property may be. In this book we're going to examine how to determine what you can really sell your house for and still come out ahead. We're also going to look at techniques for getting buyers to come to you and methods for getting offers that are acceptable. In short, we're going to see how you can get out from under that house you're in.

1
Yes You Can!

The news out there can be pretty grim, and it's coming from more than just real estate. McDonnell Douglas lays off 17,000 in southern California, and despite military needs or the Iraqi war, hires back only a fraction of them. IBM and other electronic companies cut back, faced by stiff Japanese competition. Auto sales decline for the third straight year, and workers are given long-term furloughs across the Midwest. Recession hits New England, and welfare rolls soar. In Chicago, Sears' sales drop thirty percent, and when it tries to sell its tower headquarters building, there are no takers. Over a thousand savings and loan associations are declared, by the government, to be either insolvent or not far from it. Even Chase Manhattan Bank, one of the country's largest, lays off 5,000 workers and desperately looks for capital to meet its obligations.

Just a short while back such news would have sounded like fantasy, but today it's cold hard fact. As recession takes hold, economic problems aren't limited to real estate. The whole economy is being hit. From Maine to San Diego, people, highly paid people—the ones who can afford to pay big prices for homes—are losing their jobs in record numbers . . . and can't find new ones.

Of course, the worst of the country's problems are in real estate. As noted in the introduction, sales prices are down in most of the nation. In some areas, such as New England, there are new houses that are now two years old and have never been sold! (Tract homes in Texas lost by owners to foreclosure four and five years ago are just now being resold.) Even the Japanese who bought a lot of American real estate are hurting and want to bail out, but can't find buyers for their American companies and properties.

Why It's Happening

What in the world caused the real estate crunch we're all now feeling? It surely wasn't expected. Until quite recently, it's been a seller's market. In early 1989, for example, sales on the West Coast (Los Angeles and San Francisco markets) were brisk until, one day, they just fell off a cliff. Suddenly, there were no more buyers. Why? Why did it happen? What does it mean to you?

It's important to know what's going on in the field when you sell your home and are faced with a down market. Without knowledge, too often the reaction is one of hopelessness—the tendency is to throw up your hands and say, it can't be sold.

However, if you know why things are happening, it gives you a measure of control. If you know what's happening currently, you can plan and adjust for it in the future. So, here in encapsulated form is my understanding of why the real estate market collapsed.

Fewer Buyers

There are simply fewer buyers today than there were last year or during the last decade. Far fewer people are looking for homes.

First, there's the matter of demographics. During the 1980s, "Baby Boomers," that big bulge in our population of people born immediately after the Second World War, were in their thirties, raising families. These were their prime house buying years. A lot of the pressure that forced prices higher back then came from the simple fact that these baby boomers were entering the housing market.

However, now it's the '90s, and most of these people already own homes. They aren't looking any more; they've already bought. And there are far fewer people turning thirty now and entering the housing market for the first time. In short, there just aren't as many buyers out there as there used to be.

Layoffs of Highly Paid Workers

In the past whenever the economy turned down, it was the low-paid workers who were first laid off. Companies economized by firing the mail clerk or the stock room boy. This time, however, it's different. This time the reductions are at the other end of the spectrum—highly paid workers are being laid off.

There are many reasons for this, but one of the biggest has to do with the reduction in defense spending caused by the recent changes in the Soviet Union. While reducing the Russian threat is certainly a desirable goal, the real "peace dividend" has been the laying off of hundreds of thousands of highly paid defense and aerospace workers. The list of companies laying off people by the tens of thousands reads like the Fortune 100 of high paying employers: Hughes, McDonnell Douglas, Boeing, Lockheed, etc. For the most part these were engineers and technicians, workers who could command salaries in the mid five figures—in other words, potential buyers for higher priced homes. The Iraqi war caused many production line employees to be rehired, but not those in research and development.

In addition, there are problems in Wall Street as major invest-ment brokerage houses reel under attacks of illegal and immoral practices. And then, there's simply slow business. Shearson, Lehman, Hutton alone laid off more than 10,000 employees. Again the resulting exodus has been of well-paid financiers and brokers, who were the prime buyers for homes.

In short, the very buyers who are most able to purchase homes are the ones who lost their jobs.

Lack of Affordability

Even those who kept their jobs often could not buy homes. In many areas of the country home prices became so high that few could afford to buy them. According to the National Association of Realtors®, the median priced home in the United States is around $100,000, and the median salary is about $33,000. That means only about half the people in the country can afford to buy a median priced home. In California, the state with the largest home market, it has been estimated that only about 20 percent of the population, one in five, could afford to buy the median priced home. In short, if you have a house priced over $100,000 in almost any area of the country, there are simply very few people who can qualify to buy it.

Of course, during the boom times, buyers were borrowing money from relatives to make down payments and taking on extra jobs in order to handle large monthly payments. It became a kind of frenzy as buyers pulled out all the stops to get into homes. They did this thinking if they didn't buy today, prices would only get higher tomorrow.

Of course, once it became apparent that the market was turning down that all stopped. Today, buyers are looking for less expensive housing.

Overbuilding

Then there was massive overbuilding in many areas of the country. In the Northeast, for example, 1.03 houses were built for each new buyer in the area. Imagine, if all the buyers available only purchased new homes, without any consideration for resales, there still would have been new houses left over! Add resales to the market and you find a huge surplus. To make matters worse, most builders put up expensive houses. (Land costs had risen, so it was difficult if not impossible to make a profit on a cheap house.) Top priced houses came onto the market just as high-paid workers were being laid off.

Similar overbuilding, though not as severe, also occurred in many other markets, particularly in Arizona, southern California, and Florida. (In Arizona there was a sort of contest among the state's ten largest savings and loan associations to see who could make the most residential construction loans. The result was that seven of the ten largest savings and loans in the state lost, and were forced into insolvency by their foolish actions.)

Builders were no less fooled than the bankers. They saw all those buyers during the 1980s and thought the flood would last forever. But the flow of buyers dried up. When it did, builders couldn't dispose of their often high-priced homes, so they lost them through foreclosure. Unfortunately, that didn't help the market, since the lenders, in turn, put the houses right up for sale.

Overbuilding helped create a huge surplus of residential properties that will take years to work through the system. It's going to be quite a while, in most areas of the country, before a housing shortage again causes prices to begin to move upward.

Mob Effect

And then there's the "mob effect." It has to do with perceptions. When prices were moving up, buyers were willing to stretch to get into a home because they felt it would be worth more in a short time. Like a mob they mindlessly bought up every house in sight, if not for shelter, then for investment.

Now that the market has turned, however, so have perceptions. Instead of scrimping and saving to get into a home as quickly as possible (before prices went up), with the illusion shattered, it's wait and see how low prices will go before you buy. Even buyers who are well qualified and can afford to enter the market at high levels are holding back, hoping for even lower prices in the future. And the lack of buyers only compounds the problem by causing ever more houses to remain unsold, thus forcing prices ever downward.

Tax Changes

Finally, the government contributed to the decline in real estate values. One of the real reasons that real estate had done so well, historically, was the favored treatment it had received under the tax laws. As a home owner, you probably are aware that you can deduct your taxes and interest from your income. As an investor, you also used to be able to depreciate a house rented out as an investment, and write off a "paper loss."

But this second option ended for many people with the Tax Reform Act of 1986. That legislation changed the role of investment real estate to "passive" and, for those with high incomes (starting at $125,000) who did not actively rent their property, virtually eliminated the potential deduction. What this meant was that investors began to shy away from real estate.

The biggest "hits" were taken in commercial real estate, shopping centers, malls, and industrial and office space. But it affected home sales too as some investors pulled out. It wasn't a big bite, but combined with the others, it hurt.

Never Worse

Add it all up and is it any surprise that today is the worst time since the Great Depression to sell real estate? Even back during the housing slump of 1980, there were always buyers. Prices didn't fall then, they simply stagnated and didn't move upward. This is far, far different, far, far worse.

People have always talked about when the residential real estate bubble would burst. Well, it's taken five decades, but it's finally happened. Like the tulip bulb market in Renaissance Holland or the worldwide silver market of the late 1970s, all good things eventually come to an end. That, too, has happened in real estate.

Pity the Poor Seller

Okay, so we know what's happened and have a feeling for why . . . but how does that help you? You've lost your job or been transferred, and you have to sell your home. Or you want to take your family out of a high-crime area, and you can only do it by selling. Or you need a bigger or smaller house. Or you can't afford your payments and must get out. The long and the short of it is that you have to sell, now. What good does it do to know that selling is hard because of a bigger malaise affecting real estate in general?

Does all the bad news mean that it really is hopeless for you? Does it mean that those brokers you've talked to who say your house won't sell, are right?

Have faith. It is not hopeless. You *can* sell your house. But what the market conditions tell you is that you can't do it the old-fashioned way. You can't simply call up any real estate broker, list the house, and expect it to sell in a few weeks. That just won't work in today's market.

Throughout this book we are going to look at ways to make your house more marketable to buyers. We are going to find ways to attract buyers to your property like bees to honey. In short, we are going to find ways to get that old house (condo, co-op, duplex, etc.) sold.

But before we go into these techniques, found in the following chapters, I want to offer one suggestion that you might heretofore not have considered. Here's a way that, if your situation is right, you might be able to get out from under in short order.

Buy and Sell

While it's true that there are fewer qualified buyers out there, it's not true that there are *no* buyers. People are still buying homes. And the one thing that attracts them more than anything else is a low price.

What if you lowered your price? I don't mean take five percent off the price you've been asking. I mean drop that price all the way down to where it was three years ago, before the last price hike. Drop it below what your neighbors are asking for their homes. Drop it below market. Get it down there so low that a buyer would have to be a fool not to stop, take a look, and consider buying.

I can imagine what many readers are thinking at this point: "Some advice. If I wanted to give away my equity I could do it without buying this book!"

Hold on, there's method here.

Most sellers tend to be fairly short-term in their thinking, and that thinking tends to be chronological. Today we'll do this, list our house for example. Down the road a piece it might sell. After it does we'll look for a new house . . . and so on.

What you may be overlooking is that if you need to buy a new house after you sell your current one, you may already have the solution to your sales problem in hand. It's simply a matter of looking at things differently and putting the cart before the horse, instead of the other way round.

Become a Buyer

If you're going to need to buy a new home, why not do it now, before you sell your existing house? Become a buyer. Take advantage of the good side of the market. Remember, it's a *buyer's market*. Why let all the others have the fun? Get in on some of that fun and profit for yourself.

But, you may be saying, how can I buy before I sell?

It's easy, and it can make good financial sense. Just as you will have to offer a buyer a terrific bargain to get rid of your present house, so too will some other seller have to offer you a terrific bargain to get you to buy. Go out there and find that bargain. Locate a house that you can buy for $20,000, $30,000, even $40,000 below market. Lord knows they are available in most areas.

Find the house and make an offer. But make that offer *contingent* on the sale of your current home. That means that you won't have to go through with the sale unless you sell your current house. (In a strong market sellers will balk at accepting contingent offers. But in a down market, many will grab at anything, including this.)

Now, put your current house up for sale, only mark it way down for a quick sale even in today's market. Offer it for $20,000, $30,000, even $40,000 below market.

But, you may be saying, I'll be taking a terrible loss.

No you won't! You'll be transferring your equity, whatever it may be, to your new house. The important point to see here is that you don't lose if you both *buy low* and *sell low*. With any luck, you should come out even. (The reason you buy first is to lock in that low price so you know how low you can afford to go on your existing home.)

The worst trap sellers fall into is getting hung up on price. Once you realize that price is relative, you may be able to find a way out. Perhaps an illustration will help make the point.

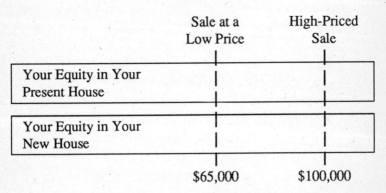

	Sale at a Low Price	High-Priced Sale
Your Equity in Your Present House		
Your Equity in Your New House		
	$65,000	$100,000

If you were able, which you're not, to sell at yesterday's high price, you might have got $100,000. But, at the time you could have commanded that price, you'd also have to turn around and buy another house also for a high price, say $100,000. In effect you'd simply be transferring your equity from one house to another.

However, today you can't sell, for example, for more than $65,000. But, presumably, you can also buy for $65,000. In other words, if you are able to offer your house at a very low price, which you can, and then turn around and buy a house for an equally low price, you are still just transferring your equity from one house to another.

Don't get hung up on price. If you're moving from one house to another, think equity. In one sense, yes, your house has definitely fallen in value in today's market.

But in another sense, no. Equity means ownership of property, and it's all on paper. If you sell low, but also buy low, you have in effect transferred your equity, whatever it might be, to another house. If the market picks up in a few years and your new house shoots back up to $100,000, you won't have lost anything! (Note: there are tax consequences to selling—see discussion below.)

Obviously this plan won't work for everyone. But, if your goal is to buy another home once you sell your current one, it could work for you. Here are the requirements for this strategy to work:

Buy/Sell Low Strategy Requirements

1. You must want to buy another home.
2. You must be able to buy that other home for a very low price. (Moving to a market where prices haven't dropped won't do.)
3. To protect yourself, you should buy first, thus nailing down the price. But you should also put in a contingency clause to protect yourself in case your present house happens not to sell. (Check with a real estate attorney for the exact wording.)
4. You must have sufficient equity in your present house to be able to lower the price far enough in order to attract buyers on price alone. (You can't sell for less than you owe, and this plan won't work if you only have a small equity.)
5. You must stop being hung up on price.

Keep in mind that this is not a fool-proof scheme. (There's no such thing.) You might buy a new home, sell your old house, and then find that the sale of your new home can't go through for some unexpected reason (the owner might have an unsalable title, or the house could be badly damaged by fire or termites). This would put you in a position of selling low but not buying low. If this happens, you'll have to scramble to get another low-priced house to buy and hope like the dickens that the market doesn't turn up before you are able to (something that doesn't seem too likely right now).

Or, you or the buyer of your house might have trouble qualifying for a loan. Or you might change your mind half way through. Or a dozen other things could go wrong.

But, then again, nothing might go wrong, and you could quickly be out of your present house and into the house of your dreams.

Tax Considerations

One final point should be noted. We've been assuming that the house you sell is your principle residence. If it is, the government allows you to roll over any gain you might receive into a new house. There are several restrictions, including the fact that to get the full roll-over your new house must cost as much as or more than your old one, and the whole process must occur within two years. There are also some nuances to the law that deal with repairs, constructions, costs, and so forth that are worth considering but are beyond the scope of this book.

Check with your tax advisor to learn the details of the law. Also look into chapter eleven.

A Formula for Success

In the following chapters we'll consider the techniques you can use to sell your home. However, before we get to those, here's a simple formula to keep in mind. It just has five steps, but each one, if followed, will help you to sell your home.

1. *Price It Right:* We'll discuss pricing in the next chapter.
2. *Make It Special:* To sell in a down market, your house must be the best on the block. Chapter five gives hints about that.
3. *Market with Flair:* You may need to offer promotional gifts or resort to auctions. See chapters four and six.
4. *Get Exposure:* You won't get an offer until buyers know your home is for sale. Get it out there in front of the public—check into chapter three for clues.
5. *Be Creative:* There are lease-options, trades, packages, partnerships, and other alternatives to consider, in chapter eight.

2
What Your House Is Really Worth Today

Value is relative. It's particularly relative to the economic times in which we live.

For example, during the period from 1975 to 1980, prices of homes across the country doubled, and in many cases tripled. It was a period of strong inflation, and real estate led the trend. A house which sold for $30,000 in 1975 might well have been worth $90,000 by 1980.

Did that house change in some way during those four years to warrant an increase in its value? Probably not. The economic times changed, money became less valuable, and people sought inflationary hedges, making the house more valuable.

Then, beginning in 1981, a real estate recession set in. Between 1981 and 1986, in most parts of the country, a house did not move up in value at all. It simply stayed the same or, in some cases, declined.

Did that house in some way change to reduce its value? Again, probably not. The stagnation and loss was externally caused by changing economic conditions. (For a detailed explanation of residential real estate cycles, I recommend my new book, *Buy, Rent And Hold*, McGraw-Hill, 1991.)

All this means is, when it comes time to sell your house, what you can get for it will be determined in large part not by the house itself, but by its value relative to economic conditions. In other words, you have to price it right for the times.

All about Price

Which brings us to price. Given the times, what is the right sales price for your home?

The oldest rule in economics is that there is a buyer for every commodity, *if* the price is right. The right price can guarantee a sale for your home almost instantly.

The truth of this can be seen most clearly when we look at commodities or stocks traded on the New York Stock Exchange, the Chicago Board of Trade, or any of dozens of other similar trading centers across the country. Gold, for example, may be offered at $392 an ounce, but there are no takers. So the seller lowers his price to $391 an ounce. Suddenly offers to buy ring across the trading pit.

Or, a stock is offered at $21^3/8$ and no one buys. So the seller instructs the broker to drop the price to $21^1/8$, and immediately someone picks it up.

The whole point is that in stocks, bonds, and commodities, all that a buyer has to do is drop the price low enough and a sale will be made. Lower the price of your stock a quarter or drop your bond a point or two and you improve your chances of selling. Drop it far enough and you find some seller who thinks it's a bargain and buys it.

The same thing holds true for real estate. Drop the price of your home far enough so that others perceive it to be a real bargain ("a steal") and you'll sell it.

However, with real estate that's not the whole truth. With real estate, price can be tempered by other factors (but not beyond the economic conditions of the times) that do not influence stocks or commodities. The truth is that price, within a fairly wide range, is not the only factor that determines a home's price. And if you want to sell your home for a reasonable price, it's important that you understand why.

Real Estate Has No Market Place

If you wanted to sell a commodity such as wheat, you would call your broker, and he would ask you how many standard bushels you had to sell. You would tell him and then ask what the price was at that moment. He would use his computer to get a quick screen of wheat futures and tell you it was so much a bushel. You might say, "Okay, sell at the market."

Your broker would then contact his firm's floor man at the exchange. There, hundreds of brokers are offering to buy and sell all kinds of commodities on a moment to moment basis. Your broker's floor man would be at the wheat pit where buyers would be yelling out the prices they are willing to pay. He would signal one of them for the number of bushels you wanted to sell, and the deal would be done. It could take less than five minutes from the time you called and be just that simple. Further, you'd be reasonably sure that you had got close to the market price for wheat at the time you sold.

However, if you wanted to sell your house and you called your broker, a good many things would be different. First, there would be no "standard" house that you were selling. Given condition, design, and location, every house is unique.

Second, there is no central market place for sales. There are no exchanges or selling pits. There is no place where buyers congregate. Rather, in order to sell you have to put up a sign, advertise, list your home, and do other things hoping that a would-be buyer will discover it.

In short, while for commodities, stocks, and bonds the price is quickly determined by brokers in a central market place dealing in standardized units (bushels, barrels, common stocks, etc.), it's different for real estate. Selling a home adds at least two additional features:

1. *Exposure*—Buyers have to discover that you have a house for sale.

2. *Marketing*—Buyers have to be convinced of the value of what you have to sell.

If truth be told, even though real estate is the ultimate investment for most Americans, selling it is more like selling a car than it is like selling stocks, bonds, and commodities. In short, in real estate the price is often determined more by the sizzle than by the steak.

Price When Selling Your Home

All of which brings us to an understanding of what price really means when it comes time to sell your home. It's not just a matter of finding out what other houses have recently sold for, although that's a good starting place, as we'll soon see. Rather, price, as well as speed of sale, is also determined by how much the buyer likes your property.

Consider: Jane and Bill both have houses to sell. They are the same model in the same tract, but on different but similar streets. Agents tell both of them that the market value for such homes currently is about $115,000. Bill lists his house and asks $110,000, $5,000 less than market. Jane also lists her house, but she asks $120,000, $5,000 more than market.

Bill simply sits and waits for an offer. Jane, however, puts in new front landscaping, paints her home, and has the carpets cleaned. In addition, she personally contacts 100 brokers telling them about her house. And she pays for additional advertising and promotion.

Just from this small amount of information, whose house do you think will sell first and for what price?

In my experience, Jane will sell faster and for a higher price than Bill. The reason, once again, is that there is no central market place where price is established for homes. Rather, every deal is unique.

All you have to do is find a buyer who falls in love with your home and you can sell for far more than the so-called market price. In the trenches it all comes down to how well you market and how well you expose your property.

That's the reason that in the chapters that follow we're going to deal in depth with techniques for marketing and exposure that you probably never hear of, but which can work for you.

First, however, we're going to talk about how you find out where to start, the estimated market value of your home. Ultimately you may get more, or less, than this figure. But you must at least know roughly what other homes similar to yours are going for so that you have a point of reference.

Time as an Element in Looking at Comparable Sales

Return to our analogy of stock investments: if you have a stock, say Microsoft Computers, and you call your broker and ask, "What's it selling for?" what you are really asking for is the market value. Your broker, in effect, goes back to the most recent sales of the stock and gives you that price. Let's say it's $50 a share.

Does that mean your stock is worth $50? Probably so, or very close to it.

Now, let's take real estate. You call up a real estate agent and he comes out to your house. He looks at your place and then tells you that comparable houses have sold for $150,000. Does that mean your house is worth $150,000?

Yes and no.

Estimating market value in real estate relies heavily on the sale of comparables. Similar to stocks, that means what the last person who sold was able to get.

But unlike stocks, where the market is liquid and you can sell in five minutes, in real estate the market is illiquid. By the time that you find a buyer, probably months after you determine a price, your house may be worth far more or less than the original market estimate.

Only a Guide

Thus, when you factor in what you do to fix up and market your home with the passage of time, you discover that estimating market value based on comparable sales is only a guide. Sometimes it's a poor guide.

This does not mean, however, that you can ignore comparable sales. The market is the market. It's true that anything is possible, and you might conceivably sell your home for $500,000 even though the estimated market value, based on recent sales of comparable homes, is $100,000. Maybe a rich foreigner will show up and decide that the alignment of stars and moon is perfect only for your house and is willing to pay a king's ransom to get it. It could happen, only I wouldn't hold my breath until it does.

Certainly, as noted, how you market your home and fix it up will help a lot, but in the real world you can't turn a sow into a diamond, and you can't sell a $100,000 house for $500,000. In fact you probably can't sell it for $125,000.

Yesterday's Prices

Looking at comparables may be unpleasant in a down market, but it has a wonderful way of bringing home the reality of the real estate market in your area. And separating reality from fantasy is important, if you really want a sale.

Ask yourself, "What is my house worth, today?"

I pose that question to a lot of people, and invariably the answer they give me is based on a price that might have been true a year or more ago, back when prices were a lot better than they are now. Almost never will a home seller give me an accurate or even close to accurate estimate of the current market value based on comparable sales.

This is not to say that sellers aren't intelligent enough to figure out current market values. They most certainly are. It's just that when it comes to value, our minds tend to play games with us.

This reminds me of a true story about an aunt of mine. Aunt Leah, when she was younger, bought one of the first color television sets that were introduced. I can't remember the exact size of the screen, but it couldn't have been more than ten inches across. And the picture was never very clear. But, it was a marvel in its day, a full console in fine maple wood sitting there in her living room. As a boy, I remember her telling me that she had paid over $2,000 for the set, and that was in the days when $2,000 was a lot of money.

As time passed I grew, and occasionally I would come back to visit. There in the living room, proudly standing in a position of prominence, was that old TV set. By now the picture had got so bad that Aunt Leah had had to squint to see what was on the screen. But she still polished it, and when company came, she would occasionally walk over and touch it so that the guests would be sure to notice.

One day, when I was still young, I committed heresy in Aunt Leah's house. I had come over for dinner and was trying to watch a football game on the old thing. I couldn't tell who had the ball, the 49ers or the Vikings. It was frustrating watching such an archaic piece of junk. So I blurted out, "Aunt Leah, why don't you get a new TV?"

She turned toward me with astonishment plain across her face. "I paid $2,000 for that set. It's the best that's made."

"That was then," I continued lickety split, without stopping to think. "Now is now. You can get a bigger and better set for $200."

She opened her mouth to speak, then closed it. She went over to the set and patted it. There was actually a tear in her eye.

In that moment I saw the error of my ways. $2,000 had undoubtedly been a huge amount of money for Aunt Leah, and she probably remembered how hard it had been earning it. When she put it all into that TV set, she felt she was getting true value in return. To her, that set still represented $2,000. I had just callously brought home the reality that it wasn't worth $200 anymore. That was something she really didn't want to hear.

"Well, at least it's got a nice cabinet," I lamely began, "and they don't build them like that anymore. It's a real heirloom. I'm sure it's worth a lot." For a moment she glanced down at the set, then turned with a smile on her face and asked if I wanted some cookies.

For a lot of sellers, their house is much like Aunt Leah's television set. They remember how hard it was raising the down payment. They can vividly recall scrimping each month to make those mortgage payments. And when prices went up during recent boom markets, they rejoiced in their newly found paper profits.

They had made a good investment. Here was real value. They proudly gazed at their house.

Only times change. What goes up sometimes also goes down. For reasons we've already discussed, housing values are declining. That paper profit may no longer exist. In fact, in terms of market price, the house might not even be worth what they originally paid for it. The $100,000 price paid for the property seven years ago might have grown to $120,000 two years ago. But today, in reality it might have fallen to $90,000.

Yet, while it's very easy to accept an increase in value from $100,000 to $120,000, for many sellers it is almost impossible to accept a decrease from $120,000 to $90,000. When the market value of something we own goes up, we rejoice. But when it goes down, we tend to hide our heads in the sand and say, "It just isn't so!"

Today's Prices

All of which means it isn't hard to determine estimated market value for your property. A little effort will get you a pretty accurate report of what comparables have sold for, as we'll see shortly. But accepting that value is something else.

I can remember over a decade ago when I made one of my first investments in precious metals. I bought gold, then in its ascendency, for about $380 an ounce. Only I bought gold futures, which meant I controlled 100 ounces or $38,000 of the metal.

Almost immediately the price dropped to $350 an ounce for a loss of $3,000. I called up my commodities broker and said, "Get me out." He replied, "Shall I sell your contract at the market?"

"No," I replied, "get me out at $380 so I won't lose any money."

There was a long pause, then a sympathetic voice said, "I'd love to do that, but the market today is $350. You have two choices. You can sell for $350, or wait hoping the price goes back up."

As it turned out, I decided to wait, the price went to $480, and I patted myself on the back at my foresight. Nevertheless, for a few moments there it was very difficult. I had become emotionally attached to a price of $380. That's what I perceived as the value of my investment, and I simply did not want to sell for any less.

An Emotional Attachment

If you are contemplating selling your house, I'm now going to ask you do to a very difficult thing. I'm going to ask you to think to yourself and decide if the price you have in your mind for your house is the realistic market price of today. Or is it yesterday's value?

If it's yesterday's value, I'm going to ask you to let go of it. Yesterday's value, no matter how much sweat, blood, and tears you put into it, is gone. Just as I couldn't get back my $380 price once the market dropped to $350, or Aunt Leah could never get $2,000 anymore for her old set, the price you might have got for your house last year or two years ago or whenever prices were high, is history. It no longer exists. Dwelling on it will only preclude you from making a sale today.

Finding Your Home's Estimated Market Value

Once you've given up your emotional attachment to yesterday's prices, you're ready to determine, as accurately as possible, what your home is worth today. How do you do that?

As I've already suggested, the simplest and indeed the best way to determine the value of your home is to examine the recent sale of comparables. Yes, recent sales aren't going to be of homes exactly like yours. But they should be of homes very much like yours. There's an easy and a hard way of doing this. I suggest the easy way, but we'll discuss both.

The Hard Way

Go down to the Hall of Records (or whatever department of your county or township keeps property records) and ask to see recent sales. All sales are recorded since this, after all, is how title to property is protected. Usually there is a list of title transfers available going back several months. (If there isn't, then you'll simply have to wade through the old records of your housing tract and those nearby yourself finding out when transfers were made— not a very appealing task.)

Once you get a list of recent sales, get the parcel number and sales date and go to the county or township assessor's office. Now look up the price of the recent sale. In most areas of the country today, the county or township assessor keeps track of sales prices in order to be able to increase the value of the property for tax purposes. (If there is no such record, then check tax transfer stamps assessed in some states. These are placed on deeds for the amount of sales price, and if you know the price for each stamp, you can quickly approximate the sale price.)

Now, armed with the prices of recent home sales, go check them out to be sure they're really comparable. (One may have a pool that you don't, another may have an added-on bedroom that you don't, and so forth.)

There's only one hitch here. The assessor's office and re-corder's office usually don't show street addresses. They typically just show legal addresses, which indicate the property on a certain map, page, and book. You'll have to look up the map in the recorder's office to find out where the houses are.

The Easy Way

Call your local real estate broker. Try to find one who has been in the business for at least five years. That way he or she should have a good feel for the market.

Simply indicate you are interested in listing your house (you don't actually have to list, of course, unless you want to—there's no obligation), and you want a free appraisal. You can be sure that the agent will be over almost before you get a chance to put the phone down.

The agent will have access to the sales prices of comparable homes sold through the Multiple Listing Service®, which exists in virtually every city and hamlet in the country, and which is almost entirely computerized. (Since this service usually accounts for between 95 and 98 percent of the sales, the access is virtually total.)

Further, the agent should be able to provide you with not only a list of comparable homes that have recently sold, but also a complete description of the homes sold, including bedrooms, baths, fireplace, pool, air-conditioning, and so forth, as well as the list price, the sales price, and maybe even a photo!

In short, everything you need to analyze comparables should be right at hand. You can simply go down the list and average out the prices, and that would be the estimated market value of your home.

Checking Comparables

As with most things in life, it's never that simple. There are basically two problems. One we've already seen is time. Typically there won't be many sales, if any, within the past few months. This is particularly the case in a down market. There may be only one or two comparable sales in the past six months to a year. And prices may have gone down since.

There is a way around this: check the median sales price of homes in your region of the country. Again, your friendly agent should be a quick source of this information.

The median price is the halfway point—as many houses sold above the price as below. It moves up or down depending on the market.

Simply find out the median price for right now and again for six months ago, then check the percentage *difference*. How far, if at all, has the median price dropped? (Make sure you figure it out as a percentage.)

Now subtract that percentage amount off the last comparable sale, and that's going to be your best estimate of your current market value.

The second problem is that no two houses are exactly comparable. The only way to find out just how close is to drive by the houses you are considering as comparable. But, you may say, you've got a complete description, even a photo. Why bother to drive by?

As soon as you do, you'll understand why. Written descriptions, even tiny photos, are never the same as seeing the property. Maybe your house is on a wonderful street of loving neighbors. But the comparable that sold has a fertilizer plant on one side and a crack house on the other. Looking at photos and descriptions won't tell you that. But these neighborhood influences will certainly affect price (probably more than anything else)!

You'll also be able to tell how the landscaping and paint look. If they're better than yours, maybe you ought to knock a few dollars off the price of your home. If they're worse, you could add a few bucks.

Nothing takes the place of an on-site visit.

Other Sources for Determining Market Value

Some sellers utilize other sources for determining value. They check the papers for open house ads and go visit the listed properties to see what other people are selling and at what price. To my way of thinking, this process is hit or miss. Besides, the asking price is one thing; the selling price quite another. When you visit an open house, you are only getting to see the asking price.

Yet another method is to hire an independent appraiser to come in and give an appraisal of the property. (Appraisers are listed in the yellow pages of the phone book.)

This may seem like the ideal choice. However, in my experience, appraisers do nothing more than check comparables, something you can do for yourself. And today, because of the overappraised values which brought down so many savings and loans, they tend to be too conservative, in my judgement. So the price they come up with may still be inaccurate. (Remember, only a buyer ready, willing, and able to purchase can determine the true market value of your property.) Finally, the cost of the appraisal is typically between $175 and $350, money better spent, to my way of thinking, on marketing, as we'll see shortly.

Procedure for Finding Market Price

1. Get comparables from an agent.
2. Adjust comparable prices for recent market moves (using the median sales prices for your area).
3. Check out the comparables, and adjust your price up or down accordingly.

Is this, then, finally the market price?

It's as close as you're going to get. Forget about checking the square footage against building costs or other methods that appraisers sometimes use. In a down market they are useless. Doing it the old fashioned way, as you have just done, is the closest you can come.

Just remember, it's an imperfect method. Whether you use the hard way or the easy, it's not the same as trading stocks, bonds, or commodities at an exchange. There the market price is known moment to moment. With real estate, it's always a guess. An increase in interest rates will tend to drive prices downward. The announcement of a plant opening and new jobs in the area should shift prices up. Other factors, too, will affect price. You can try to account for these, but it's all guess work; there's no scientific method to it.

After You Find the Market Price

Now, you're ready to do better!

In the next few chapters we'll look at how to sell for more than the so-called market value by getting more exposure for your property and by making it more marketable.

3

How to Get Good Exposure for Your Home

If you write a book and want to plug it on the Johnny Carson show, how do you get on? Or if you're a new entertainer and you want to appear on the Arsenio Hall show, how do you get through to Arsenio?

Or if you're running for public office and you want your name and ideas to appear on the front page of the local paper, how do you manage that? Or if you're opening a new restaurant, how do you let people know where you are and what you serve?

You could leave it all to chance. You could hope that Johnny or Arsenio or the local newspaper editor or the restaurant reporter will hear about you and call.

If you do, however, you could be waiting a long, long time for that phone to ring. Publicity normally doesn't come looking for you. Consider TV talk shows. When guests appear on them, the host usually acts like they're long lost friends having a wonderful reunion, saying isn't it marvelous that they've finally had a chance to get together and chat here on television. The truth is that the guest appearing has usually mounted a clever and sometimes massive campaign in order to get that appearance on the show.

The guest either directly or through a publicist may have called the show's producer, its host, mutual friends, even advertisers in order to secure those precious few moments before the camera. The same holds true in courting a newspaper editor or writer: the publicist may know someone on staff or may actually write an article for the paper. The politician may "stage" a political event solely to gather media coverage. The restauranteur may offer lavish free meals to the reviewer.

The whole reason, of course, is exposure. You could be the greatest comedian in the world, but if no one knew that you were appearing at the Comedy Club and nobody showed up to watch you, you'd die. Or you could have written the greatest novel or "how to" book, but if no one knows about it, it'll sit on the bookstore shelves until the dealers send it back. Or you could have the greatest political program, but if the papers never report it, you won't get many votes.

The key to success in virtually any field is exposure. And knowing how to get that exposure is the key to the key. In this chapter we're going to look at how you can get exposure for your house. Just like the author or the entertainer or the politician or the restaurateur, you have something you want to promote—your home. The question for you is, how do you get to those people who might want to buy? How do you get exposure for your property in order to get a quicker sale at a higher price?

Hiring an Agent

Personalities hire publicists, as we've noted. The first step for most sellers is to hire the equivalent of a publicist for your property. Hire someone who will go out there and get to those potential buyers, letting them know what you have to offer. Of course, I'm speaking of a real estate agent or broker (the terms are synonymous). (We'll discuss selling your home by yourself shortly, but first let's consider the advantages of a good agent.)

When someone in entertainment hires a publicist, what he or she is looking for is a high-powered person with connections who can get publicity. Unfortunately, when many people hire a broker, they often don't have such high expectations. Most sellers, in fact, simply anticipate the broker will put a sign in front of the house (something you could easily do for yourself and for far less than the commission you're going to pay), that he will advertise the property (something you also can do, again for much less than the commission), and that he will bring by any buyers who happen to call.

And that's about it. Most sellers anticipate that in doing these three things, the agent will somehow dig a prospective buyer out of the woodwork.

In fact, in a good market that often happens. Many times when the market's active all that's needed is to put a sign out and list with an office. There are so many buyers around that one or more is likely to stumble onto your property.

However, it's a different story in a down market. In a down market there are thousands of houses and only dozens of buyers. The odds are definitely stacked against you, and you need something more than a sign and an ad. You need a true publicist, someone who can do the equivalent of getting you on Johnny or Arsenio's show. You need someone who gets exposure for your house among all the thousands of other houses competing for attention.

In a down market the single most important feature of agents (assuming, of course, that they are honest and competent) is that they know how to get exposure for your property; that they know how to place your property before prospective buyers.

The Trouble with Agents

Finding a real estate agent who's also a publicist, however, can be difficult. Here's why: Let's say you're selling your house for $150,000, and you're going to pay your agent a commission of 6 percent. (Commissions are negotiable, and nationwide they typically run between 5 and 7 percent.) That means the agent is going to get $9,000 if the property is sold. However, if the property doesn't sell, the agent gets nothing.

One would think this would be a strong incentive to the agent to move forward publicizing your property as much as possible. A $9,000 commission, after all, is nothing to sneeze at, even in this day and age.

If you believe this, then you really don't understand how agents handle their business. (I've spent many years as an agent and can assure you that only one seller in a hundred really understands his agent.)

Agents think in terms of "staying alive." Staying alive means not only making deals, but also keeping expenses low, especially in a down market. In real estate, the agent who lasts is one who "turns off the lights" to save on electric bills when no one's using the office.

Deals, especially in a down market, are few and far between. On the other hand, expenses come in regularly and can be pretty stiff. There's an office and car to maintain, furniture to buy and upgrade, phone lines to pay for, as well as sufficient advertising to buy to make that phone ring. (Brokers pay for all of the above; salespeople work for brokers and don't get a salary but must provide their own car, clothes, and, most expensive of all, time.) It's important to keep in mind that all of these expenses come about before the agent spends a dime extra specifically on your particular property.

(For information on how to handle a listing agreement with an agent, as well as a discussion of which agent will serve you best, and the types of agents and brokers who are out there, I suggest my book, *Tips And Traps When Selling A Home,* McGraw-Hill, 1990.)

A Word about Broker Advertising

Agents do advertise, and that's a regular expense. However, it's important to understand that the ads the agents place are intended to bring potential buyers and sellers (who will list) to the agent. They aren't really intended to sell a specific property.

Once in the office, the agent will attempt to swing those buyers to whatever house he thinks they might buy. There is almost no loyalty to the house that was originally advertised. An agent will show any buyer who comes into his or her office any property the agent thinks the buyer will purchase.

Extra Exposure for Your House

All of which comes down to this important fact: most brokers either aren't willing or don't have the resources (particularly in this market) to get extra exposure for just your house. Further, if you pressure them, they may refuse to spend any additional money on your property. They have two good (for them) reasons:

First, in a down market they have many, many properties available for sale besides yours, and only a few buyers. Keep in mind that most brokers are linked to a Multiple Listing Service®. Although they personally (or their office) may only have a few dozen properties listed, through the MLS they have access to thousands of houses. True, when they sell an MLS house they'll have to split their commission. But they almost always figure it's better to split a commission than to miss a sale. When a buyer comes into the office, your agent may mention your listing first. But as soon as the buyer indicates a preference for something even slightly different such as location, size, features, the agent will open that MLS book and start hunting.

Second, for the agent, spending extra bucks on your house may be like throwing money down a bottomless pit. What if that agent spends just a thousand dollars extra on advertising your place? (Keep in mind that the agent is already putting up the cost of the sign and the fee for listing your house on the MLS, which might amount to a few hundred bucks.) Your house is just one of thousands for sale. What if it doesn't sell, something that's very likely in a down market? Now your agent is out a thousand dollars (plus the original couple of hundred), with nothing to show for it.

But, you may point out to your agent, that's taking a pessimistic viewpoint. What if it does sell? What about the big commission—doesn't that make the extra expense all worthwhile for the agent?

Most of us are pretty savvy when it comes to our own money, and agents are no different. They know the odds, and they play them. They know, for example, that it is rare in real estate that the person who lists a house will also sell it. In better than 90 percent of the cases, different agencies list and sell. That means the actual money they are likely to receive in a sale is far less than you might think.

Commission Splitting

Let's say your agent spends an extra thousand dollars promoting your property, and then, as most often happens, an agent in a different office sells it. The commission is now split between the two offices.

The splits vary from fifty-fifty to sixty-forty. If it's a sixty-forty split, your agent's *office* gets just forty percent of $9,000 or $3,600.

Further, if your agent happens to be a salesperson, he now has to split with his broker. If this is a fifty-fifty split he now gets $1,800. Imagine, the listing agent may only get $1,800 of a $9,000 commission.

But he's spent a couple hundred on the sign and the MLS. And if you've somehow got him to pop for an additional $1,000 promoting your property, he's in for perhaps $1,200.

After his expenses (including an extra $1,000 which he may have spent on your home), he's made a grand total of only $600. Now he has to pay for his own regular expenses, such as car (gas, depreciation, maintenance, etc.), phone, and, of course, time.

In short, if the agent spends a thousand dollars extra promoting your property, and even if the property does sell, he stands to break even at best. If the property doesn't sell, something very, very likely in a down market, he's out a thousand bucks or more.

The long and the short of it is that 99 percent of real estate agents simply can't afford to spend the money it takes to get the proper exposure for your property. They simply would lose money if they did.

So how do you get proper exposure for your property?

Offer to Pay for Some Exposure

One way is to pay for it yourself. After all, who's more interested in a sale than you? It's important to understand that in real estate virtually everything is negotiable, and that includes the terms of the listing agreement.

Most listing agreements simply specify that the agent will work diligently to find a buyer. How he does that is up to him. In a normal market this works out fine. Typically there are more than enough buyers to go around, so that in a reasonable amount of time, one or more will bump into your agent and, one way or another, a sale will be made.

In a down market, however, things are different. Here you need to do something extra to get that house of yours out front. My suggestion is that you offer to pay for some of that extra exposure you need. (We'll discuss just where the money is to go in a moment.)

Thus, why not say to your agent, "I'll list this property with you for three months (I always suggest a three month listing—less time is too short to get results, more time is not warranted) *if* you'll agree to give it an extra push. I want results and I want exposure, and I'm willing to pay for them. I'll make you this offer.

"I'll put up $1,000 towards the promotion of my property. If the house doesn't sell, I'm out the grand. It doesn't cost you, Mr. Agent, anything. On the other hand, if it does sell, you lower your commission by $500. In other words, we split the cost of promoting my property."

Most agents will leap at this opportunity. Here's a seller wise enough to know that promoting a property costs money and who is willing to pay for it. What have they got to lose? If it doesn't sell, they're out nothing. And some of the promotion you do may bring in other buyers or sellers to them. If it does sell, it has cost them only $500.

There's a big advantage to you, too. You can be sure the agent is promoting your property above others because of the extra bucks you're putting in.

Further, you have little to lose. If you're serious about selling in a down market, you've already contemplated lowering your price. So lower it in the form of $500 (assuming it sells and the agent pays $500) spent on promotion. (You'll probably pay more than that to have it painted or the garden renovated.)

But what if it doesn't sell, you may be asking?

It's important for you to think positive. You're going to put up a grand because you want to sell it, because you're a motivated seller. If you're just playing games and listing to test the waters, certainly don't spend the extra bucks. And certainly don't be surprised if it doesn't sell. But if you're committed to getting a sale in a down market, you have to go to extraordinary lengths, you have to go the extra mile. Remember this old adage: if *you* don't believe it will sell, who will?

Where to Spend the Promotion Money

Once you've decided to spend some money promoting the sale of your home (a hard thing to do), and once you've found an agent who's willing to work with you on this (a very easy thing to do), the question naturally arises: where are you going to spend the money? After all, a thousand dollars is not a king's ransom. It's not exactly going to buy a great deal of attention. However, sometimes it's not how much you spend but how wisely you spend it that counts.

First off, be sure the arrangement you have with the agent is something like this: Yes, you will throw a thousand dollars into the kitty to help promote your property. But no, you're not going to give a penny of that money to the agent to spend. (If you did, how would you know the money was spent on your property and not on the agent's overhead?)

Instead, you work out an arrangement (and put it in writing) that you and the agent are going to coordinate for certain types of events or exposure, and that up to your commitment of $1,000, you'll pay for them directly.

Here are some suggestions of what you might do. You don't have to do all of the following, but you might want to do one or more. They may all get you extra exposure.

Drinks and Snacks for Caravaners

It's important to understand how real estate agents learn about properties other agents have listed on the cooperative listing service. Typically dozens to hundreds of new listings (depending on the size of the area covered) come out once or twice a week. If they come out on Monday, for example, the agents will go through the sheets and pick out those that are most likely to sell, or that fill the need of some buyers with whom they will be working. Then the agents will tour those homes.

Since there are lots of offices and lots of agents in those offices, these tours become a sort of caravan. In fact, in some areas, the local real estate board will actually organize a caravan tour to stop at various homes.

The caravan is the first and one of the most important ways your agent can promote your property. Yes, when you list your property, a description and usually a photo appears in a book that nearly all agents have access to. But it's just one of thousands of similar listings, and unless there is something special about it to catch the agent's eye, it will get nary a second glance.

You need to make your house stand out in the minds of as many real estate agents as possible. You want them to come by and see your property. What's more, you don't want them to just peek in and pop out. You want them to stick around for a few moments and

begin wondering if maybe your house will work for one of their
buyers. In short, before you sell the buyer, you first have to sell the
agents.

One very effective way to do this is to offer a champagne and
snacks stop on the caravan tour. Every other house will simply be
a quick stop for the agents. But, if they realize they are going to get
drinks and food, you can be sure they'll stop, look, and *remember*
your place.

Keep in mind that agents often get treated badly by sellers.
Sellers usually only complain that agents take too long to sell,
don't advertise enough, and bring buyers by at unreasonable
hours.

You be a different kind of seller. Cater to the agents. Offer them
food and drink and they will be there, in droves. They will linger
awhile, and maybe one of them will remember a buyer who is
looking for just what you're offering.

Cost? Probably under $200. The champagne doesn't have to be
expensive, and the food can be just cheese and crackers. It's the
thought here that counts. Check with your listing broker to see how
many he or she anticipates will show up.

Board Presentation

In addition to having the real estate agents come by, there's
another means they have of letting each other know about "hot"
properties, those they think will sell. Each real estate board in an
area (to which almost all agents belong) has a weekly meeting.
Here, each member can stand up and tout a piece of property.

You want your agent to stand up and tell the other agents present
(often they number in the hundreds) about the wonderful opportunity to make a commission that your property represents.

Only your agent has to have something special to say. He or she
can't expect to catch the ears of savvy real estate brokers with
puffery such as, "It's a beautiful, gorgeous place." Or, "It shows
very well" (meaning that when the agents bring prospective

buyers through, the property looks good—something that most agents say of most properties). Or, "The seller is very anxious." Every seller is very anxious in today's down market.

Your agent has to stand up and be able to say something that those listening can take to the bank. Here, as in most other areas of business, money talks. You have to give your agent some ammunition. For example, here are some highly motivating things your agent can say that will definitely catch the ears of other listening agents:

My seller has authorized me to say he will pay a $1,000 bonus to any agent who can bring in an acceptable offer within the next two weeks.

This isn't going to make agents try to switch buyers from a house they really want to your house. But, it will let them know that you are *highly motivated*, two words that mean potential sales to them. Also, if they are given the choice between showing your house and another or recommending your home over another, your can be sure they will remember that $1,000 bonus, and it could very likely play a role in their decision.

My seller has authorized an increase in commission.

As an alternative to a lump sum bonus, you could also offer to pay a higher commission. If the typical commission in your area is six percent, you could offer six and a half. On a $150,000 house you're only speaking of $750 more. Yet, that $750 might make the difference between a quick, good sale or a prolonged and ultimately unsuccessful sales period.

My seller will offer a free trip to Hawaii to the agent who brings in a buyer!

This sounds like more than it really is. A five day, four night trip to Hawaii usually can be arranged for under a thousand dollars, depending on the area of the country and the quality of the trip. Yet, it's a perk that will perk up the listener's ear, particularly if it's offered during the winter months when it's snowing outside (and, incidentally, when it's harder to sell property).

Your goal at these board meetings (which, by the way, you, as a seller, are normally not invited to attend) is to drum up interest in your property among those who walk with buyers. These are three ways guaranteed to do it.

Special Advertisements

Thus far we've talked about motivating your agent. Let's move on toward helping your agent directly in hooking buyers.

In real estate, besides word of mouth, the best way of getting exposure for your property is through space in the local paper. That's where buyers look. That's where agents advertise.

When you sign your listing, you should insist that one of the conditions which must be met by your agent is that they agree to advertise your house *every week* in the local paper. The agent is going to advertise anyway, so it might as well be your property. (You don't want to list with a broker who doesn't advertise.)

If you insist upon this, most brokers will balk. They will point out that they know best when it comes to advertising and you should leave it to them. They will sometimes advertise your property and sometimes other properties. But, they will always be trying to swing buyers toward your house.

Baloney! The ads are intended to get any and all buyers (and sellers) in the agents' doors, and then the agents will sell whatever property they can. Remember, most agents have little to no loyalty to the ads the buyer originally calls about.

However, you don't care about people coming in the door of the agency or about other houses. You only care about your house, and you only want yours advertised. Maybe you'll be lucky and someone who calls on the ad will like your place and will buy it. It's an opportunity you don't want to miss out on.

However, since most brokers will balk at taking a listing that specifies how they will advertise, you may be out of luck... unless you offer to pay for part of the ads.

Cooperative Ads

Cooperative ads (where the seller and the agent split the cost) are done all the time in virtually every other field. Book publishers often pay half the costs for an ad placed by a bookstore. Tire manufacturers often pay a large portion of an ad run by tire dealers. Electronics manufacturers pay a percentage of ads run by retail outlets, provided their equipment is featured. It's done all the time in hundreds of other areas. Why not real estate?

Of course, advertising can be expensive. You want to limit the amount of money you're committing to. On the other hand, one ad of half a dozen lines or so in the Sunday paper isn't going to break the broker's bank, or yours.

If you agree to pay for half or a portion of the advertising provided your house is featured, you're going to get the broker's attention. Of course, that doesn't mean you should do his or her job. You can also stipulate that if the house sells, the broker is to pay you back for the advertising. Most brokers will go along. They have virtually nothing to lose and a great deal to gain.

You Pay for Ads

The problem with any ads is the lack of broker loyalty to the house being advertised. Yes, when a prospective buyer calls about your home, the agent may extoll its virtues. But, at the first hint that your house may not be exactly what the buyer wants, the agent may turn to other houses. After all, the agent isn't so much interested in selling your house as in selling *any* house.

So why not pay for the entire ad yourself and use your own phone number? You answer the calls. You field the questions. You then refer interested buyers to your agent for screening and showing the house.

This has both advantages and drawbacks. The advantages include the fact that you'll know immediately how well your ad is doing. You'll also be able to really puff up your house and get a buyer excited. And you'll know that only your home is being promoted.

The disadvantage may be that it will cost you not only advertising money, but time. And you may not be as good at selling a buyer as your agent.

Nevertheless, I think it's worthwhile.

By the way, your agent may object and say he won't allow advertising unless his name appears. Fine. Agree to put his name on the ad. As long as it's your number, and you identify yourself as the owner and not an agent, it shouldn't matter.

Further, the agent may say he's afraid you're trying to steal a commission away. This is a phony argument. If you sign an "Exclusive Right To Sell" listing, upon which most brokers insist, you pay a commission no matter who sells, you or the agent. (Again, check into my book, *Tips And Traps When Selling A Home* for an extensive discussion on listing.)

Writing the Ad

One last point: what you say in the newspaper ad can be critical. Simply another ad puffing up another house will be passed over quickly by savvy buyers. (A savvy buyer is one who knows it's a buyer's market and is only interested in a good deal.) Here are some ideas for ad lead-ins to catch the buyer's attention:

The Seller Is Paying for this Ad!

It can then go on to say that you're so determined to sell this house, you're helping to foot the cost of the advertisement.

I'm a Motivated Seller!

Really? Buyers are going to wonder how motivated. The ad should go on to say just what you're willing to do that other sellers aren't.

Agent's Choice!

The agent chose to advertise your house over others. (I wonder why!)

There are many books out on successful print advertising and how to write good lead-ins. But don't overlook the resource that your broker offers. He or she has undoubtedly been putting ads in papers for a long time and may have an excellent idea of what attracts buyers (and what doesn't) in your area.

Time on Cable TV

Here's an area almost completely missed by real estate agents, yet which provides a wonderful opportunity for you. Most metropolitan areas of the country have cable television, and the cable companies usually run a channel that gives local information, such as the time and programming. These companies also often offer the channel to people who want to feature special events, such as Little League or AYSO Soccer. And many of these companies also will sell time at a very reasonable rate for advertising.

They may not be willing to sell ads directly to agents, but they very likely will sell a spot to you. Typical rates are $25 for twenty-five seconds several times a week.

If you have a camcorder or can borrow one, you can easily put together a quick ad touting your house. If you only have a 35mm camera you can take a color picture and blow it up, then do a voice-over describing the property. It doesn't have to look professional. In fact, the more amateurish it looks, the more likely it is to catch viewers' attention. (It will stand out amidst all the polish of professionally produced TV, and people will wonder what you have to say.) This can be a lot of fun and can generate enormous exposure for your home.

Of course, you can put in the broker's phone number, and alert him or her to expect a flood of calls on your property. Well, there may not be a flood. But all it takes is one call, if it's from the right buyer.

One word of caution: Expect to be copied. You may be the first kid on your block to try TV to sell your house, but you can be sure others watching who also want to sell will be quick to jump on board, particularly if it gets around that this technique snared a buyer. Of course, if you've sold by then why should you care?

Signs on Billboards and Posters

The sign on your house is effective in letting everyone know it's for sale. (One of the hardest properties to sell is one in a country club or other restricted setting where no "For Sale" signs are allowed.)

However, the sign in your front yard will only be seen by those buyers who happen to cruise by your neighborhood. Additional signs placed on vacant lots (with the owner's permission) at cross streets or put on posters hung in local shops will enormously increase exposure. Be sure the sign describes your property and tells how to get to it.

Your agent can handle the additional signs placed on vacant lots. He'll have to contact lot owners, but usually something can be worked out. And you can usually work out a deal where you'll pay half the costs, which are often negligible. (It's positively amazing that this sort of thing is done so little. Suggest it to a broker and most will jump at the opportunity. But few will bring it up on their own.)

Signs in store windows are tricky. Most businesses would resist a request from an agent. But you, as an individual, may have more luck. Be prepared for rejection. But occasionally a friendly store owner may comply. Just be sure your poster looks really good and professional, or the store owner as well as potential buyers will reject it out of hand.

One device some owners are using in conjunction with agents is the "Open House" sign. Many agents will spend their Sundays sitting at houses with "Open House" signs in front and on intersecting streets. You can expect your agent to do this once or twice for your property, but you can't expect him or her to do it all the time.

But you're there all the time, and there's no reason why you can't borrow the agent's signs and place them strategically so passersby will see them on weekends or whenever you're available. You can show the house and get potential buyers interested. The agent can take over from there.

A word of caution here: Whenever you advertise your address you are not only attracting potential buyers but also exposing yourself to criminals. You could be marking your house for burglary. (Brokers, at least, attempt to screen buyers before bringing them by.)

Whether you want to advertise your house with signs and run the risks is a judgement call you'll have to make. In some neighborhoods it's no problem at all. In others, it's simply not a good idea.

Selling by Yourself

By now I'm sure some readers are saying to themselves, "What am I paying that agent a commission for? If I have to do all the work, why not simply sell the property myself?"

If you think you're the first seller to consider saving the commission by selling your home yourself, think again. Every seller thinks this. Yet, statistics indicate that fully 95 to 98 percent of homes are sold through agents. Nevertheless, you can do it. Methods of selling by owner are detailed in chapter seven. Here, however, let's consider the idea from the perspective of marketing and exposure.

Probably the most difficult aspect of selling a home yourself is getting the proper exposure. Remember, when the market's strong, buyers are driving around just looking for properties they can bid on. However, when it's down, they tend to become very independent. The agents, through the Multiple Listing Service, offer you enormous exposure. That, after all, is the main reason people list. Can you overcome this?

No. If the truth be known, you can't. You can never give your property as much exposure as a real estate agent can bring to it through cobroking (working with other brokers). But through the techniques we mentioned earlier, newspaper advertising, TV ads, bulletin boards, signs, posters, and so forth, you can let people know what you have for sale. And maybe, just maybe, that's enough. Remember, you don't have a hundred houses to sell, or ten, or even two. All you've got is one, and all you need is one buyer.

Therefore, if you're motivated enough to give up your week-ends, face buyers who are offering you $50,000 less than you're asking, and all the rest, then by all means go for it! Why not try to sell it yourself?

What's Needed to Sell on Your Own

A Good Looking Sign

The days of the old metal stake in the ground with a masonite sign bolted to it are long gone in most areas of the country. Today, signs are usually four-inch by four-inch posts stuck in the ground with a sign suspended from a horizontal beam. The signs are typically well designed, look good, and blend in with the decor of the neighborhood. (Many communities even have sign ordinances restricting the type of sign you can use.)

Brokers use these new signs, but they don't build them or even put them into the ground. Instead, this function is normally carried out by a local sign company. Usually that sign company will do for you what it does for the brokers. You can call your local real estate board to see if they'll give you the name and phone number of their sign guy. (Surprisingly, many will!) Or you can look under "Signs Made" in the yellow pages.

The sign guy, however, will have two charges. The first is for the sign itself (lettering, paint, etc.). The second is for the post that holds the sign and for putting it into the ground.

A good sign will cost you $50 to $75 for the post and ground insertion and another $100 or so for lettering and painting. All of a sudden you're out $175. But, if you sell you'll save a hundred times that on commission. (On the other hand, if you don't sell . . . but why be negative?)

What to Say on Your Sign

The next question is what you should say on your sign. Quite frankly, the most appealing words you can use to hook a buyer are, "For Sale By Owner." These words always catch a buyer's eye since he or she thinks they portend a bargain. Also, buyers know yours is a house that brokers, with whom they have been dealing, aren't likely to show them. If they see the sign, it's a sure bet they will think about stopping.

Unfortunately, every agent in town who sees the sign will also stop by. To avoid a parade of agents trying to list your property, some sellers will add, "Principles Only." This tells brokers you're not interested in listing, and may keep some of them away.

Of course you'll also want to put your phone number on the sign and make it large. A buyer may be driving by at twenty-five to thirty-five miles an hour, and he or she will miss tiny letters.

With any room left, you'll want to indicate size (bedrooms and baths), and any special features, such as pool, spa, air conditioning, fireplace, etc. That's about all you will have room for.

One last recommendation with regard to price: Don't put the price on your sign. It will scare away more buyers than it attracts. Further, you may be willing to negotiate and a price won't tell that to the buyer. If you want to put something on the sign suggestive of price, put, "Make Offer" or "All Reasonable Offers Considered." This will appear inviting to potential buyers, and may encourage them to stop by and make an offer.

Advertising

We've already covered this. It's the same when you sell by owner as when you use an agent. Don't forget posters and flyers as well as cable TV plugs. (If you're willing to pay a broker to do it, why not pay yourself to do it as well?)

Technical Aspects

Of course, there's always the technical aspects of the sale, the paper work. If you've sold houses before, you'll know what to expect and this won't bother you. On the other hand, if this is your first deal, secure the services of a competent real estate attorney. That person can draw up the sales agreement and handle all the other paper work for you.

Alternating Selling by Yourself with Hiring an Agent

As with most things in life, we are all really interested only in results. It ultimately doesn't matter whether you sell yourself or by an agent, *as long as the house gets sold!*

What you want to avoid is wasting a lot of time on an agent who doesn't get a buyer or, similarly, wasting a lot of time trying to sell on your own and not being able to find a buyer. You want to sell as soon as possible and not waste any time.

My suggestion here is that you alternate both methods. Use a broker and, alternately, try it yourself.

For example, you may list with a broker for three months. If your house isn't sold within that period, you may then want to try selling it yourself for, say, another few months. If it still isn't sold, you can go back to the broker.

Alternating has certain advantages. It offers you the opportunity to get the exposure a broker can bring. It also gives you that chance to sell by yourself and save the commission.

I would caution against simply deciding to sell by yourself and proceeding to do so indefinitely. You could spend years trying to sell and for one reason or another never find a buyer. Alternating offers you the best of both worlds.

Phone Services

Several organizations have started in various parts of the country that, for a fee, will offer a description of your property to prospective buyers. For example, a buyer might call an 800 number and get a recording describing a dozen or even a hundred homes, one of which is yours. Or another system offers a listing of houses for sale by owner including descriptions and photos.

These services offer an additional means of getting exposure. However, their value at this writing is not proven. Few buyers know about them and use them. They may become a force to reckon with in the future, but they are just a gimmick so far.

4
Auctions

We've all seen or been to an auction at one time or another, even if only on television or in the movies. An audience of buyers sits before a raised platform on which an auctioneer, usually speaking rapidly and loudly, extolls the virtues of whatever he or she happens to be selling. It could be Persian rugs or Iowa wheat. The auctioneer cajoles, pleads, bullies, or otherwise attempts to get the buyers to put up their hard cash and make the purchase.

The function of the auctioneer, in fact, is not just to get buyers to bid, but to bid higher. The word "auction" is derived from the Latin *auctio*, which literally means to increase (the value). The auctioneer, presumably, can sell something for more than an owner can.

For their services auctioneers sometimes accept a set fee. Other times they want a piece of the action. Usually, the better the auctioneer, the higher the fee.

Auctions in a Down Market

When the real estate market turns down as it has, sellers will go to extraordinary lengths to get out of their properties. One method that is cropping up more and more is the auction.

Currently home auctions are being used primarily by builders. Auctions rarely work when there is only one item being sold. But a builder has a whole tract of dozens, maybe hundreds of homes. Hence, the auction works well.

Today, builders from California to New York are engaging the services of auctioneers to get rid of unsold properties. They hope the auction will result in a quicker sale at a higher price than they could get for themselves.

Of course, here we're not concerned with builders, but with you as an individual. Yet, with certain restrictions, you too may be able to take advantage of an auction.

Individual Home Sellers and Auctions

As a home owner your big disadvantage when it comes to an auction is that you have only one item to sell, your home. That doesn't mean that you can't contract with an auctioneer to sell it— you can. It does mean, however, that your chances of getting a good sale are limited. A lot has to do with psychology.

At an auction, one of the key elements is the heightening of the audience's emotion by the auctioneer. All buyers come to auctions assuming not only that they will be able to find something they need, but that they will get it at a bargain price. Consequently, when they walk in the door they tend to be guarded. They're not going to spend a dime until they see fifteen cents worth of value.

However, once the auction begins and buyer bids against buyer, emotions can overcome reason. I have seen buyers who at the beginning of an auction wouldn't bid ten dollars for an item, and an hour into the auction offer thousands of dollars in competition with others. It's sort of the same thing that happens when you go to the casinos at Las Vegas or Atlantic City. The auction breeds a kind of excitement where the buyer begins to think he or she might have the chance of a lifetime to get a bargain . . . yet might miss out to others if he or she doesn't bid quickly and higher.

Passions ride high at auctions, and I have seen buyers come close to fisticuffs when things went against them. Of course, the auctioneer is doing his or her darndest to get just this sort of thing going and growing.

But working an audience into a buying frenzy at an auction requires a large number of items to sell. The auctioneer has to build the buyers up just like a comedian works a cold audience into a hot one. You can't build enthusiasm with only one item to sell.

(As a result, you usually don't want your item, house or whatever, to be the first sold, because it will almost always get the lowest bids. Rather, you want it to be sold toward the end of the auction, when the buying fever is running the hottest.)

The "Leaving Town Auction"

As I said, the big problem is that you as an individual only have one item to sell, in this case, your house. However, there are two ways you, as an individual home owner, can overcome this problem. The first is the "Leaving Town Auction." The second is the "Combination Auction." We'll look at both.

The Leaving Town Auction is a glorified garage sale. You promote that, for whatever reason, you are moving away, and want to get rid of all of your valuables, including your house. You get an auctioneer, and you sell off everything, from the refrigerator to the beds to the piano.

The whole point is to have a variety of things to sell. You want the auction to last at least an hour so that buyers get sufficiently worked up to be willing to pay big bucks. Of course, you only sell the higher priced items, so that buyers with big wallets are attracted. And the finale is when the auctioneer sells the house.

Does it work? Sometimes.

The key to the Leaving Town Auction is getting the right buyers to attend. If the only people who show up are curiosity seekers and your neighbors, the sale will be a flop. Similarly, if only buyers who are interested in household furniture show up, the sale won't work for you. Yes, the furniture may get sold, sometimes for a very healthy price. But if your house isn't moved, the whole point of the sale has been defeated.

What it really takes for a Leaving Town Auction to work is to get house buyers in the audience. You want people to attend who are actively looking for homes. You also want real estate investors there. In short, you want as many people as possible to show up who have both the ability and the desire to purchase your home. Those who also come to buy furniture will have their chance. But their whole purpose is to create a buying fever for the others.

How to Get Home Buyers to Attend

It's not that easy to get real home buyers to attend, but it can be done. The key, of course, is exposure. Keep in mind that you have a number of things working for you. The most important is that people today know real estate is down, and thus there are going to be all sorts of opportunities to get good deals. They may never have personally attended an auction before, and yours may be the first held in their area, but they will still come, even if for no other reason than to satisfy their curiosity. Maybe they will find a house they'll want to buy, maybe not. But they may feel that the whole thing could be well worth seeing. (Never underestimate the spectacle attraction of an auction. It may be the most exciting thing to happen in your neck of the woods in the last month!)

Things to Do to Attract the Right Kind of Buyers:

1. *Let your local real estate agents know about the auction.* Further, let them know that if they represent a buyer at the auction who eventually purchases the property through them, you'll pay them half the usual commission rate. (For example, if the commission is usually 5 percent, you'll pay them $2^{1}/_{2}$.)

You can be sure the agents in town will spread the word. Unless they have a buyer hooked on a specific piece of property, they'll mention yours. After all, if they cobroke a property through the Multiple Listing Service, they stand to get only half a commission, so why not work on your auction? If you let enough agents know, you can expect a good crowd represented by them and their clients alone.

2. *Put up signs and posters well in advance of the auction.* Try to put them at places buyers might go, such as banks, loan offices, and real estate companies. Just ask if you can stick up your poster. Many offices may decline, but others may agree. Be sure to give the time and place as well as a list of items to be sold. Be sure your literature clearly states that the big item is the house and that buyers must come with cashier checks or cash in hand for a deposit in order to bid.

3. *Try the local cable service.* For a small fee, perhaps $25, you may be able to run a bulletin announcing the sale.

4. *Take out a "House Auction" ad in your local newspaper.* Put it in the section where homes are listed for sale in your area. The ad does not need to be big. You just have to get across the idea that a house will be auctioned off, where and when.

Remember, at an auction, the more the merrier and, generally speaking, the better the price. You want to get a lot of potential buyers in attendance so they will see one another, talk to one another, and begin to feel the urge to get their bid in.

The Examination Period

No one these days buys a pig in a poke. Everyone wants to see what they're getting. Thus, you'll have to arrange for a period of time during which any potential buyers can look at your house, examine the terms you are offering, and make a decision on whether or not they want to bid.

Don't look at this examination period as a disadvantage. Actually, it's to your advantage to have it. The news of the auction may attract potential buyers who otherwise might never hear of your property. When they examine it, one or more may decide they really like it. And there's nothing to prevent them from making you an offer before the auction. You might actually sell your property just on the news of the auction!

If that should be your good fortune, then just accept the sale and cancel the auction. A few people might be disappointed, but you will be very pleased.

Be sure to note in your ads and literature that your house is open for inspection at specified times. Make these as broad as possible, and include evenings and weekends. You want to attract people, not scare them away. (Of course, you'll want to take precautions to prevent your property from being burglarized.)

Arranging for the Auctioneer

The big difference between a Leaving Town Auction and a regular auction by a professional auction house is that, with the former, you are actually staging the sale. You take care of getting people to attend. You arrange for the location of the auction, usually your back yard. You provide any goodies, such as champagne, cokes, cookies, etc. You rent chairs, and get the podium for the auctioneer to stand on. You may even arrange for a loud speaker system, although many auctioneers bring their own.

It's also up to you to arrange for the auctioneer. You can find their names in your local yellow pages under "Auctioneers."

Auctioneer Prices

Their prices are negotiable. They may simply want a single fee ($250, $500, or more), often half up front and half afterward. A lot depends on the auctioneer. Or they may want a percentage of the amount sold. Ask several to see what the going rates are in your area.

Note: Be wary of an auctioneer who wants both a percentage and a large fee. That way the auctioneer can't lose: if nothing sells, he still gets paid, and if your house sells, he gets paid more. There is little incentive for the auctioneer to try to work the audience up into the kind of buying frenzy that gets you the most bucks.

Hard Money Auctioneers

Some auctioneers will ask for a piece of the hard money. "Easy" money is what you could easily sell your house for on the market without the auctioneer. "Hard" money is anything over and above that amount. The auctioneer has to work to get the hard money, and there is really nothing wrong with paying him a piece here. After all, the more hard money he gets, the more money you get.

If I were auctioning off my house, I would prefer a hard money fee. This way, if the auctioneer doesn't do a good job, he gets paid less. But, his incentive is to do better, because then he'll get more, and so will I.

Frequently, however, with only one house, the auctioneer won't want to risk not making anything, and may insist on a set fee. Again, you may have to go with this. I would beware of an auctioneer who wants both a *high* set fee and a piece of the action.

Be sure you get the time and place straight with the auctioneer, and he guarantees to show up. (You don't want to end up auctioning off your house yourself—you may not be wonderful at it!) Also find out what kind of special arrangements he wants (loudspeaker, lectern, or whatever).

Determining the Terms of the Sale

When you sell your refrigerator, you only sell for cash. But when you sell your house, you simply aren't going to be able to sell for cash. The buyer will have to come up with both a down payment and a mortgage. As a result, you can't sell to just anyone. You need qualified buyers. How do you get them?

The way this is usually handled is to prequalify the potential buyers. For example, at most professionally run auctions the auctioneers insist that the bidder put up a deposit plus agree to a credit check before the auction. For example, the potential buyer has to come up with $1,000 in cash or a $2,500 cashiers check, or whatever. The money is paid to the auction company, and immediately after the sale applied toward the purchase for the successful bidder.

As an individual, this is difficult for you to do. However, you can insist on an earnest money deposit in cash or cashier's check from any successful bidder. The terms of the sale can be spelled out, in advance, in a contract which prospective buyers are invited to examine. (It can be all filled out except for the price.) The contract can specify that the deposit is non-refundable if the buyer fails to complete the sale. This doesn't guarantee you a completed sale, but it does go a long way toward assuring you only qualified buyers are likely to bid.

You will certainly want to work out the document arrangements as well as the specific terms of the sale, especially with regard to the deposit, with your real estate attorney. (You should have a real estate attorney working with you in any event.)

In addition, you can have runners up: the two or three next closest bidders can be invited to submit contingency bids. You will accept their bids, in order of highest offers, if for some reason the successful bidder can't complete the sale. (This way, if the successful bidder can't or won't buy, you don't have to hold another auction to find another buyer!)

Setting a Reserve Price

You can only sell your equity in your house. If your house has a $50,000 mortgage on it, you can't sell it for less than $50,000. Below that point, the bank owns it!

Therefore, you must set a reserve figure below which the house will not sell. For example, you may feel your house is worth $100,000 in today's down market. Your mortgage is $50,000. You hope to get more than $100,000, but in any event you will not sell for less than $90,000. You instruct the auctioneer to hold the house in reserve if no one bids more than that.

The trouble is that most buyers don't like to come to reserve sales. Knowing there's a reserve takes the excitement out of the sale because buyers know prices can't fall below a certain point. Therefore, some professional auctions will just casually note (in fine print) that there's a reserve. Some unscrupulous auctioneers will actually say that it's an "absolute" sale, meaning there is no reserve, and then just be sure not to sell below a certain price. In an extreme case they may even have a conspirator in the audience who agrees to shout out a minimum bid, thus keeping the price up.

These unfair practices are illegal in most states. Usually you must specify if there is a reserve, and if you say the sale is absolute, it must be.

The trick is to set the reserve low enough to entice buyers into thinking there is the possibility of a real bargain, and at the same time keep it high enough so you won't get hurt if there's only one bid at the reserve price. It can be tricky, and you should discuss it with your real estate attorney and your auctioneer.

If Your House Is Already Listed

This really shouldn't be a problem. Just explain what you want to do to your real estate agent. Perhaps you can negotiate with him or her to throw in part of the commission to help offset the costs of the sale.

Having the house listed can actually be a bonus, as the real estate agent will be able to give you valuable advice on handling buyers, and will also be able to "talk up" the auction to other brokers and, thus, get more potential buyers to attend.

If your broker refuses to go along, then you may just have to postpone the auction until after your listing expires. (It's unlikely your broker will object, since an unsold house in a down market is not a listing to treasure.)

The Combination Auction

Admittedly, the Leaving Town Auction is a tricky thing to pull off. No matter how you attempt to disguise it by selling off furniture and appliances first, there is still only one house for sale. If no one starts off the bidding for the house, you may not get a sale.

The way around this, for creative sellers, is the "Combination Auction." Here you as a seller get together with other individual home sellers and hold an auction of many houses. If you can get as many as a dozen sellers to go along, you can throw an exciting auction where you can all profit.

The key to the Combination Auction is finding other sellers who are willing to go along. In a normal market, this would be difficult. But in a down market, it should be far easier.

Finding Other Participants

The first place to look is with your agent. If you've listed with an active agent, he or she should have lots of other listings as well. Approach your agent with a proposal: you'll help sell all of that agent's listings in one grand auction sale!

Some agents are too rigid and old-fashioned even to hear of such a thing. But others will quickly pick up on the idea. In fact, they may grab the ball and run with it. After all, think of the commissions they could make if in one Saturday afternoon they could sell ten houses, especially in a down market!

If you work with the agent, the procedure is similar to the one I described for the Leaving Town Auction. However, either you or the agent must get together with the other sellers and have them agree, in writing, to holding the auction and to their reserve prices.

If you don't have your property listed, there's no reason why you still can't throw a combination auction. However, here you'll pretty much have to organize it yourself. (You won't get much help from agents if they're not getting a commission.) Your best bet will probably be to contact other owners who are selling by themselves.

You do, however, have one big advantage here. A sign which reads, "For Sale By Owners—Auction!" will surely grab a lot of attention, and will probably command a good audience.

Organizing the Auction

After you find a group of sellers who are willing to hold a combination auction, organize a group discussion in one of the sellers' houses. Also, someone familiar with the auction process is a good guest to invite. Try having the auctioneer show up.

You can expect other sellers to have many questions and to be wary of the idea. After all, in a normal sale they have strong control over the negotiations. A buyer makes an offer and they can accept or counter-offer. At any time before they accept the offer, they can pull out of the negotiations.

Here, they are being asked to give up much of that control. Here, they are being asked to consign their house to an auctioneer with the hope that they'll get a good price. They know that if things don't go well, they could get a bad price. It's about this time that the matter of the reserve usually comes up.

Getting Other Sellers to Set a Reasonable Reserve

Many sellers, wary of being cheated, may say, "My bottom price is what I've got the house listed for. Why should I go any lower?"

At this point some explanations of how auctions are run and some convincing about why it's important to set lower prices is in order. Reasons shouldn't be hard to find. Here are several:

Reasons for Setting a Lower Reserve at an Auction

1. In a down market your house could sit unsold for months, maybe even years. An auction could provide a quick sale.

2. The reserve is the *minimum* price you will accept. It is the enticement to the buyers to come to the auction. Setting the reserve doesn't necessarily mean that this is what you will actually get, but establishes the absolute minimum you will take.

3. Most sellers don't really think they will sell for the listed price. Usually they understand the buyers will make lower offers and in order to sell, particularly in a down market, they'll have to come down 5 or even 10 percent. Why not do that now for the auction?

4. It's a down market. Your house is sitting unsold. If you must sell it and get out, how much do you really have to lose by trying an auction? At least it's an opportunity.

5. You may get more than you think. Don't dwell on the possible downside. Look also to the upside. If the auctioneer is good, the buyers are eager, and you have some luck, you could get more than you originally had expected to get.

Given the opportunity for a quick sale, most sellers will jump at the chance. However, be sure their commitment is in writing and there is an auction document among you, other participants, and especially the auctioneer. Also, you'll want the document approved by your real estate attorney. You don't want an unhappy seller later coming back and claiming you talked them into selling for less than they wanted to get for their property, or that they really didn't understand what the auction entailed.

Everyone Contributes

It's important to understand that although the idea of the auction may come from you, the cost should not be fully borne by you. In order to be successful, everyone should contribute equally. This ensures the other sellers are committed and won't pull out the day before the sale.

The commitment doesn't have to be much. A few hundred dollars per seller ought to be enough to cover the staging costs, and an arrangement could be worked out that only those sellers whose houses sold would be liable for any commission to be paid to an auctioneer. (At a Combination Auction, the auctioneer is likely to want a piece of the action. Just be sure that you don't give away too much. If you're listed with an agent at 6 percent and you agree to give the auctioneer 5 percent, you're giving away the store! As noted earlier, a compromise can usually be reached where the auctioneer's fee may come out of the agent's commission.)

What if the Property Sells before the Sale?

Any auction arrangement in which you participate should contain an escape clause for you. It takes time to stage an auction whether you're the one doing it or someone else is. A month is quite fast. Sometimes it could take several months to get an auction off the ground. During that time you could get lucky. Someone could make an acceptable offer on your property. You want to be sure that if this happens, you can be excused from putting your house up for auction with no penalty to you. (You may lose the couple of hundred dollars in seed money, but that's hardly a big loss.)

As noted earlier, be sure there is an auction agreement that spells out the conditions for withdrawal among you, the auctioneer, and other participants. This is another area for your attorney to check carefully.

What if It Doesn't Sell?

If your property doesn't sell at the Combination Auction, you're really no worse off than before, except for any seed money you may have advanced. And you could be better off.

Chances are a lot of buyers came by to see your home. Some of these, while not bidding at the auction, may remember your property, come back later to see it again, and eventually make an offer. It may turn out that you will sell your house a month afterward because of the exposure it got at the auction.

The only worry is that some buyer may now regard your reserve as the price from which to start down in negotiations. But, you can always refuse to sell if you don't get your price.

Agents also benefit from an auction. If there's an agent involved, he or she will have the opportunity to make contact with other buyers, some of whom may purchase other properties. You can point this out to balky agents who don't want to go along with your auction plans.

When You're Contacted by an Auction Company

Thus far we've been discussing auctions where you are the sponsor, in one form or another. It's your idea, and either you stage it or you get others to work with you in staging it.

Auctioning off houses, however, can be big business, and as the market spirals down, more and more auction houses and auctioneers are getting into it. One day you may get a call, either directly or through your agent, asking if you want to participate in an auction being staged by someone else.

Here the tables are somewhat turned. Now you're the outsider coming in. What should your reaction be?

It should depend, of course, on how the auction is to be handled. Now you'll be asking the questions about reserve and about the level of your commitment.

When an auction house comes to you, be especially careful with regard to the amount they are to receive. When you stage it with other sellers, everybody is pretty much in the same boat, and there's less chance of one party attempting to take advantage over another.

When an auction house stages it, however, it can be expected to extract as much for itself as possible. It's here that you may run into the fee plus commission. The auction house may also want not only fee and commission, but a part of the hard money as well. This is usually considered unethical.

What's important to remember is that each case is different. You have to look at the figures for your house and see if they add up to profit for you. If the outside auction house is legitimate and competent, it may well be worth it to pay them extra money to find a buyer for your home.

Should You Sell at Auction?

There are no guarantees that your house will sell at an auction or that you'll get the price you want. But, in a down market, it's very hard not at least to consider auctions as one more option.

5

Clean and Paint

There are two truths when it comes to getting your home ready for sale. They are quite simple, yet immensely important:

1. Buyers Have No Imagination.
2. Sellers Can't See Faults

Consider the first. Do buyers really have no imagination? Well, of course they do. But when it comes to getting your property cleaned and polished, so you get the quickest sale and highest price, you have to act as though they don't. For example, you can say to buyers, "Yes, the carpet is a little ragged, but imagine what this room would look like with new carpets!" Or you can point out, "Sure the cement in this patio is a bit cracked, but add some red bricks and a cover and can't you see how good it would look?"

Oh, of course buyers can imagine and see how it would look. But not at the price you're asking. Drop your price $40,000 and sell your property as though it were a "fixer-upper," and they'll go along. But try to get top dollar (whatever that might be in a down market), and you've got buyers with no imagination.

What it comes down to is what you're selling. Are you selling a finished product or one that requires additional work? The price of a finished house differs substantially from that of a fixer-upper. Replace a ragged carpet with a new one for $1,000 and you might add $5000 in value to your property. Fix some broken concrete and add a deck cover and the same thing could happen.

In the Buyer's Mind

Buyers are always thinking about what they would do to make the place liveable, how to fix it up the way they would like it to be. When they move in they might rip out your new carpet because they don't like the color. Or they might break up the concrete deck to put in a spa.

But what they pay you and whether they make an offer really comes down to what they see right now. What is the whole product you are offering? Is it complete, or will they have to spend some more money to fix it up after they buy it? (Buyers often double the actual cost of fixing up and reduce their offer by the same amount.)

Finally, some buyers really don't have any imagination. They see what's there, and their minds don't expand to imagine what could be. They have to be shown, led, spoon fed.

In short, for you as a seller the rule always has to be that you never leave anything up to the buyer's imagination. Rather, you must always clean and paint and fix up so that what you have to offer is clear to see for all who come to look.

Spending Too Much

When prices were rising, you could easily spend $5,000 to $10,000 improving a kitchen or bath and hope to get that money back and more when it came time to sell. But in a down market, it's almost certainly a waste. Spend lots of bucks improving features of your house and you're throwing money down a bottomless pit.

In a down market buyers are nervous about price. They want to be sure they don't spend so much that they lose equity when prices fall again tomorrow. Consequently, they tend to want to offer much *less* than the last similar house sold for. In this kind of market, any sort of real improvements you make are simply not going to bring back the dollars they cost.

On the other hand, cosmetic changes are certainly going to be appealing. Remember, you want to make things clear, not leave it to a buyer's imagination. Here's what you can do:

If your house is kind of dull, paint it, or at least paint the front. The same holds true inside.

And keep the place spotless, especially the kitchens and baths. If there's any black mold growing around the shower, clean it out. Do the same for the toilet, tub, and sinks. It won't cost much more than a little elbow grease, and it will present your house in the best light.

Dealing with Appearance Problems

Of course, sometimes a dab of paint and a rub with a sponge won't do it. Maybe, for example, your house is an old cracker box. But it's in an area where new houses have been built that are selling for $400,000. Does that mean your house, even in a down market, will bring close to that high price?

Probably not. Those who look at your house are probably expecting grandeur, not tiny bedrooms and cracked walls. They may be expecting a large kitchen with a cooking island, not a small railroad car kitchen with the sink one body-width away from the stove. They may be looking forward to expansive grounds, not a weed bed in the back yard.

In short, buyers may discount the entire value of your house. They may think to themselves that the house is hopeless, so what you're really selling is not much more than a vacant lot. And they'll offer you a vacant lot price, perhaps half or less than what you think the property is worth.

Improving the Appearance

What you need to do to get your money's worth out of your home is to improve the appearance of your property to the point where a buyer is willing to make that leap of imagination, willing to accept as credible that your property is indeed worth $400,000. In short, you may need to spend some bucks to make the house look worth the price.

But, how much should you spend? We just said that in a down market, spending big bucks was throwing money away. How can you afford to spend a large amount of money now to improve the appearance of your home?

(Of course, your house may not be worth $400,000. But even if it's only a $40,000 house the principle is the same. How can you justify spending even a thousand dollars upgrading it when the market is down?)

The answer is that in some cases you may need to spend the bucks just to get the sale at a price that's anywhere near reasonable. Not spending the money may simply mean no sale at all or offers you can't accept.

It comes down to a matter of necessity. You don't want to spend money improving . . . but you may have to.

How to Know if You Need to Improve Your Property

This gets us back to the second truth of fixing-up: Sellers can see no faults.

This is not to say that you as a seller are blind to problems with your property. But the tendency is to overlook them. After all, if you're living there and it's good enough for you, why shouldn't it be good enough for a buyer?

However, what we are willing to live with may not be saleable. I can recall one couple living in a house which had very low water pressure because of rusted pipes. Because of the expense involved in replacing those pipes, that couple was willing to accept showers where the water barely dribbled out.

However, when they went to sell, they ran into trouble. Buyers would turn on the faucets and immediately realize there was a problem. (The real estate agent told them that, to protect themselves against a possible later lawsuit, they should divulge the water pipe problem.)

The cost of repiping the entire house was $3,500. They told buyers this was the case and said they would be willing to knock that amount off the price.

But buyers couldn't seem to see the house with the water pipes fixed. All they saw was a house with a problem. So, instead of worrying about fixing the pipes themselves, they simply looked elsewhere. (In a down market buyers can afford to be finicky.)

Finally, in order to sell, the couple had to bite the bullet and fix the pipes themselves. It was a $3,500 risk, but in their case it was the only way to get a sale.

You may have a similar situation. It may not involve pipes, but could involve any other aspect of the property. You may need to make repairs in order to get a sale. But as I said before, your own perception may not be the best guide. You may be willing to live with something that no buyer will tolerate.

Therefore, I suggest that you get an outside opinion as to what serious work, if any, needs to be done to get your property into shape. You don't want just anyone's opinion, however. You want an educated perspective.

The first logical place to start is with the real estate agent. He or she may be able to tell you quickly what you can get by with and what needs to be corrected.

However, my own observation is that agents really tend to see only the work that needs to be done to bring your home up to the standards of similar homes. If there's something unusual that might be done that could give a big boost to the price you might get, they might overlook it. Therefore, I suggest you consult two additional sources: an interior designer and an architect.

Talking to an Interior Designer

Your motivation in talking to an interior designer is to get ideas. You may or may not use the designer. (Perhaps you can work out an arrangement where for a nominal fee the designer will present ideas to you with the understanding that you won't buy furniture through him or her.) But his or her ideas can help you decide on colors, furniture arrangements, panelling, and even adding room dividers.

Don't sell this kind of planning short. You may have lived in the house for ten years and think there's no better way to fix it than you currently have it. However, a designer could come in and in a few moments make suggestions that would add enormous appeal (and bucks) to the house.

Sometimes having lived in it for a long time can be a real disadvantage. We tend to get set in our ways and overlook obvious changes that could easily be made for the better.

Remember, it's important to understand that the interior designer is not going to help us buy new furnishings or redecorate the house. Why would we want to do this when we're planning to move? The purpose here is to improve the interior appearance, and for that the designer can be invaluable.

Talking to an Architect

An architect can do for the outside of your house what a designer can do inside. He or she can make suggestions and give you ideas for changes that could significantly alter the appearance of the property (particularly that all important "curb appeal," or the first sight of the house the buyers get).

But, I hear some readers saying, I don't intend to rebuild the home. Why should I spend money for an architect?

First off, it's important to understand you're not asking for a set of drawings or plans. You're only asking for ideas. Perhaps you know someone who's an architect who can help out? A local college or university can also be a resource, as they may be able to offer a student in architecture. Or, you could simply agree to a nominal fee for the architect's ideas.

Secondly, we're not talking about making any kind of major additions or changes. For example, recently some friends wanted to sell their home in an area where houses were going for $200,000. However, most of the houses were newer, while their house was over thirty years old. The problem they faced was convincing a buyer to overlook many of the house's old-fashioned architectural features.

The architect knocked on the door and announced right off the bat that their entrance way was the worst feature a buyer would see from the outside. It had a couple of posts supporting a small cover and then just three steps leading to the house.

He pointed out that today's homes were usually designed with an entrance way. The more elegant the entrance way, the more valuable prospective buyers were likely to perceive the property to be. With just the three concrete steps, the house looked old and a bit out-of-date.

The sellers said they saw what the architect was saying, although the entrance didn't bother them. But, they certainly didn't see spending thousands of dollars for a new entry.

The architect said it wasn't necessary. He recommended a magazine which had recently published a series of articles on entries. It showed how to use wood (redwood or cedar) to create an entry porch that was wide and quite pleasant. It also described how to put a small wood screen over the top to give it a sense of elegance and privacy. Finally, a couple of old wooden tubs with bright flowers finished off a now elegant entrance.

The sellers thanked the architect and went for it. They did the work themselves, buying the wood for a couple of hundred dollars. Inside of a few weekends they had a spectacular new entrance to their home.

Once again, it's not that you want the architect to do any major work for you. What you want is someone skilled and trained at looking at houses to give you some new ideas. The architect should be able to isolate problem areas immediately and then offer solutions. Of course, it's up to you to carry them out.

Putting Your House in Order

Yes, you want to fix up the old place so it looks its best. No, because of today's down market you don't want to spend any big bucks. The answer lies somewhere in between.

Of necessity, most of the work you do will be cosmetic. But even cosmetic work can make a world of difference. Simply adding paint and a few bright flowers to a front will add dollars and appeal to your home.

The real key, however, is to get the right advice and then to act on it. Find out what a professional (interior designer or architect) would do. After all, they make their living doing nothing but making property look good.

Then, act on it. My suggestion is to do nothing that isn't absolutely necessary (like fixing the plumbing), especially big ticket items. And remember that even a small amount of money can often make a world of difference.

6

Promotional Giveaways that Sell Homes

We've all seen those TV game shows where contestants win prizes (not cash, but such things as cars and jewelry) by answering questions or performing some sort of stunts. I'm sure you know the kind of show I'm talking about.

For a moment now, I'd like you to consider how those shows actually work. In other words, what causes viewers to tune in and turn on to them? Is it the questions that are being asked?

I'm certain there is a certain intellectual competition that we all feel with the contestants as we try to get the answer before they do. But, I don't think that's the real motivation.

There's also the spectacle of the show itself. Average people such as you or I get up on stage right next to stars and models. Perhaps we can see ourselves there. But would we watch just for this? What's the actual motivation for watching these shows?

Consider the prize awards themselves. Sometimes they are cash. But very often they are expensive automobiles or cruise vacations or television sets or other consumer items. Have you ever noticed how much time out of each show is spent showing off the items that can be won?

I'm no psychologist, but my suspicion is that the real hook those shows use to catch viewers is the glamour of the prizes. When we tune in, we dream about winning those prizes ourselves. How wonderful our life would be with a new car or a cruise or even a new set of dishes.

In short, the TV game shows, to my way of thinking, sell fantasy. That's what most viewers tune in to watch: average people like you or me winning wonderful prizes.

Whether you agree with my pop psychology or not, there can be no question that the prizes take up a big part of the show, as much as a quarter of the viewing time. Nor can there be any question that the shows are popular. They've been around since television started, and before that on radio. (Does anyone remember "Queen For A Day"?)

What does all this have to do with your selling your house? Simply this: it may be possible for you to latch onto the glamour appeal of those giveaway shows in order to get rid of your property. In other words, you may be able to capture the fantasy by doing the same sorts of things the game shows do.

Why Use Giveaways?

I'm sure many readers are saying to themselves, "Surely he's not talking about giving away a car or a cruise or a TV set when I sell my house. That's ridiculous."

Yes, that's exactly what I am suggesting, and, no, it's not ridiculous. Further, if you do it right, it's not even that costly. And it could make just enough of a difference to get someone to look at, and make an offer on your home. In this chapter we're going to see how you can offer giveaways that will draw buyers in and make some of them want to purchase your property. First, however, let's get past some misconceptions.

Misconception #1—"No one will be interested."

There's the story of the seller who sits in his easy chair listening to his real estate broker propose that maybe he might want to offer a bonus or an award to prospective buyers in order to induce someone to make an offer in a down market. The seller listens while the broker explains the concept, then he laughs. "I'm trying to sell a house. Why would anyone be more interested in the house if I throw in a TV set or a car? They know I just have to add the price of those items to the cost of the house. They'd rather just have a lower price."

This seller is still sitting there waiting for a buyer.

Selling real estate is no different from selling anything else. Yes, you must have some steak to offer. But you also have to let the buyer hear the sizzle.

We've already talked about how buyers have little imagination. They have to be shown what a place can look like before they "see" it. Similarly, in a down market, they have to feel there's something special about the house they are going to make an offer on, or they'll look elsewhere.

Think of it from the buyer's perspective. As a buyer, you walk into the house. You're looking at this and at that, and the house seems okay, but no different from a dozen other houses you've seen. Then the agent (or the seller), opens the garage door, revealing a late model, highly polished car. "By the way," the agent mentions, "if you buy the house, the car goes with it."

"What!?" you exclaim. "You mean the car is part of the house?"

"Yes," the agent teases, "It fits so well in the garage, the sellers decided to throw it in."

"This I have to see," you gasp and walk over to the car. It's only a year or two old, in mint condition. Maybe you don't need a car. But, you could always use another one. And with the seller throwing in the car, he must be really determined to get rid of the property. This is a place you'll seriously want to consider making an offer on. Maybe you'd better look around more carefully to see if this house really can fit your needs. And so on . . .

Never underestimate the fantasies of buyers. Cater to them and you have a better chance of selling.

Misconception #2—"No one else is giving away anything, so why should I?"

Do yourself a favor. For one weekend, pretend you are a buyer. Go to new houses that are for sale as well as resales in the price range of the house you are trying to sell. See what's out there. You might be very surprised.

While you probably won't find too many sellers offering awards or bonuses (some probably will be), you may find this sort of thing heavily done by builders. New home builders are basically marketers, and they won't pass up any chance to improve their sales. If a new car in the garage or a microwave in the kitchen or a TV set will hook a seller, they'll use that hook.

In short, you're not the only one doing this. In fact in some areas, particularly the Northeast and the Southwest, you may find there are a great many sellers doing this. You may have to offer some sort of award just to keep up with the other sellers!

Misconception #3—"It costs too much."

This is the biggest misconception of all. The cost of awards is frequently only a fraction of what it appears they must cost. The reason, quite frankly, is that few people know what items actually cost.

Let's take a car for example. You want to throw a car in with the sale of a house. Let's say you don't want to throw in your own car (although if you have one you want to get rid of, this could be a great opportunity), but for the sake of argument, you're going to buy one. How much will it cost?

For openers, let's eliminate new cars. They are very pricy, and for a bonus, most buyers won't really quibble if the car is only a year or two old. Instead, let's consider a car that's got perhaps 15,000 miles on it, is two years old, and is in great shape. How much will such a vehicle cost you?

First of all, keep in mind that it's not just housing that's in a recession right now. The auto market, particularly the used car market, has never seen worse times. The Kelly Blue Book price of cars (used to determine wholesale and retail prices) has rarely seen market prices go down faster. A two year old car, in some cases, can be purchased for half or less of what a new car costs. (Something to consider when you're in the market to buy a new car.) Let's say you want to offer a Chevy or a Plymouth or a basic Ford that costs around $15,000 new. Chances are you can find a two year old version for $6,000 or $7,000.

Or if a car is too expensive to consider, what about a TV? You can buy a giant screen television set for under $2,000, a wood veneer floor model that's thirty inches big for under $900. What about setting one of these beauties up in the corner of the family or living room and throwing it in with the price? Relatively few people have one, but most people want them. Again, you might think no one will buy a house to get a TV set. Of course, not. Yet, it's something with which to hook a buyer, to get his or her attention. With the TV thrown in (or the car), they might consider your house more seriously. If it's a choice between your house or a comparable without a TV, they might opt for yours.

And then there's the cruise. If you think the automobile and housing markets are bad, you should consider the cruise markets. Some ships are leaving port only half filled.

Contact a good travel agent. Ask about a cut-rate one week cruise to anywhere. You may be astonished at the low cost, even for two people. $5,000 may buy you a wonderful cruise award.

Or what about a year's worth of maid service. Or a gardener for a year? How much can it cost you?

Finally, there's always the microwave. For a couple of hundred bucks, you can throw in a microwave. Only, be forewarned: in many markets, landlords are throwing in microwaves in order to get their homes rented. You might find that you're competing too low.

Misconception #4—"I can't afford it."

How much will a giveaway really cost you? Above, we noted that the cost will probably be between $1,000 and $10,000. You may feel you've already lowered your price on your house to below what you feel it's worth. Adding a promotion just lowers it further. You simply can't afford to do that.

If you feel this way, then I suggest you ask yourself how much it will cost you not to sell. What about those payments you have to keep making? What about your inability to move to another home? Finally, are you really serious about selling?

You may be surprised at the answers. You may find, of course, that you'd rather not sell than bother with the hassle of a give-away. If that's the case, and you're financially able, take your house off the market for now. You're wasting your time.

On the other hand, if you answer that you're deadly serious about selling, then you will also find that you may not be forced to offer a giveaway promotion. To understand why, let's consider a different area of real estate that was popular a few years ago: time-sharing.

Time-Sharing: An Example of Giveaway Promotion

Time-sharing, as it was practiced, meant a developer put together a resort or apartment complex and then, instead of selling units outright, sold the right to use them for blocks of time, usually a couple of weeks. The buyers, for example, could use the condo for two weeks in the summer, or one week in the summer and one in the winter, or some other combination.

Because of the abuse of charging too much, and because of other problems involved in time-shares, such as maintenance and management costs, most have not been successful for buyers. But the promotions used by developers to lure buyers were successful.

Perhaps you were enticed by an offer such as this: "A free weekend at Vale (or Tahoe or wherever) for two, just for attending a ninety minute presentation." Or, "You may have won a car, a boat, luggage or a camera. Just show up at our resort and listen to a ninety minute presentation to collect." Of course, the presentation was a sales pitch to get you to buy the time-share. The giveaway was the hook to get you there.

Did people show up? You bet they did. One time-share project with which I'm familiar got several hundred curious potential buyers each weekend to drive 200 miles through the desert to a distant resort to collect the giveaway prizes. Their sales rate (converting visitors to hard buyers) was above 30 percent!

I would wager, in fact, that less than one in ten of all time-shares would have ever been sold without the use of giveaway prizes. The reason, quite simply, was that no one wanted them! A demand had to be created, and that's what the giveaway did. It created a demand so buyers would show up.

That's exactly what you're doing when you offer an award to potential buyers of your home. Whatever you give away helps create a demand for your home, a demand in a market where there is virtually no demand.

When I hear a seller say, "I can't afford to offer a bonus giveaway" in this market, what I'm really hearing is, "I don't want (or don't need) to sell my house."

In short, you can't afford not to consider the idea of a bonus in this market.

Misconception #5—"I can't do it because I don't have the cash."

You don't need cash. Consider what is probably the highest priced giveaway you can offer, an automobile. Should you go out and buy a car so that you can give it away with your house?

That would be foolish. You only need the car when the house sells. Until then, you only need the appearance of the car. Some sellers will work out arrangements with local used car dealers where, for a period of time, they can keep a "for sale" car in front of their property (or in their garage) with the understanding that if and when the house sells, they'll buy the car from the proceeds.

Would a used car dealer do this in a strong auto market? Probably not. But in today's market, it's a different story. Today, with cars as depressed as houses in some areas, a dealer might be willing to do it. And if he won't, an individual seller (found through ads in the paper) might. There's no end to the kind of deals that can be put together in a down market.

You can rent a TV set. Yes, you actually can. Check your phone book. There are rental companies which will rent anything, including big-screen TVs. Of course, renting suggests you don't really think your house will sell. If you're serious and believe 100 percent in the sale of your property, you can always get a TV set on credit and pay off the debt from the sales money.

A cruise won't cost you anything until you buy it. And you don't have to buy it until your house is ready to close escrow. (The price of the cruise, in fact, can be paid to the travel agent directly from the escrow funds.)

Misconception #6:—"It will reduce the money I receive for my house."

Offering a giveaway bonus could reduce the cash you get back. But, it could also increase it.

Think of it this way. In today's market, realistically speaking, you're not going to get what you may consider the best price for your home. (As noted earlier, this typically is the highest price a house comparable to yours sold for in the past few years.) You're going to have to cut your price, somewhat, in order to get any kind of a sale.

The real question, therefore is not whether you'll need to cut your price, but by how much. (We'll have more to say about price cutting decision making in a later chapter.) What I'm suggesting is that you'll need to cut your price less with a giveaway bonus than without one. Further, you will significantly increase your chances of a quicker sale. Perhaps an example will help.

Let's say your house at the market peak was worth $280,000. However, recently houses like yours have been selling for closer to $220,000.

Unfortunately, buyers coming into the market don't want to purchase a home only to see the price fall even lower. So they are making low-ball offers of around $200,000 for homes. What are you likely to get for yours?

Well, assuming there's nothing extra to make your house worth more, you can reasonably expect to list for $220,000, and after a period of time (perhaps six months, perhaps longer) accept a low-ball offer of $200,000. (You'll sell for less if the market drops further during the time your house is for sale.)

On the other hand, let's say you throw in a bonus, a cruise that will cost you $5,000. You put your house up for sale at $220,000 with the giveaway.

Buyers come by. They are enticed to see your house in the first place because of the bonus. And once there, they pay special attention to it because they figure that if it satisfies their needs, and the price is right, why not take advantage of the cruise offer?

Sooner or later (probably sooner if you or your agent promote the bonus actively) a buyer will make an offer. But, what is this buyer likely to offer? Is it the low-ball $200,000, or is it more?

I suggest the buyer of a house with a bonus is likely to offer more initially and to come up with more later on as you counter-offer back and forth. The reason has to do with buyer's motivation.

Buyers' Motivations

Buyers are motivated by a variety of things. Obviously they need a place to live; they may have to get in soon because of job or school obligations; or they may simply be tired of looking. But, basically, there are two motivations you need to consider: Greed and Love.

The worst kind of buyer is the one who offers exclusively out of greed. He's offering to purchase your home simply because it's a bargain. However, a bargain for him is not one for you. His profit is your loss. If the only way you can induce a buyer to make an offer is by cutting your price to the point where it's so low that it's a bargain, you may sell, but you'll also lose a great deal of money.

The best kind of buyers are ones who fall in love with your home, who simply feel it's the place for them and they can't live anywhere else. This kind of buyer will pay any price to get your house. Obviously, this is also the kind of buyer you want.

In the real world most buyers have both motivations to greater or lesser degrees. What you want is to motivate your buyer more with love of your house than with greed over a bargain. The bonus giveaway helps in a variety of ways:

- It brings in potential buyers who might otherwise skip looking at your property.
- It gets buyers to consider your home seriously instead of just quickly walking through.
- It gets buyers off the subject of just talking money. Your bonus isn't money, it's something a person can *dream* about: a car, a TV, a cruise, or whatever. Once they get to dreaming about the bonus, they may very well begin dreaming about the house. They may begin to see themselves living there.

That is, the bonus giveaway may motivate potential buyers to get past the inertia and fear that keeps them from making an offer. If they really like the place, and they really want to buy it, I feel they are likely to make a higher initial offer. Further, if you reject their initial offer and counter, I believe they are more likely to accept your counter offer, or at least to counter back at a higher level.

In short, the bonus giveaway will encourage buyers to move forward with making an offer and with making a better offer both initially and later on during negotiations. They will do this because you will have tapped more closely into their love than into their greed.

In our above example, let's say you end up selling for $210,000. That's $10,000 higher than you might have got without the bonus giveaway. After subtracting the bonus's cost, chances are you're still ahead. Even if you break even in terms of cost, the quicker sale should be worth a great deal to you if in no other area than in peace of mind.

Misconception #7—"It limits buyers."

Some sellers think just because they're offering a bonus give-away, a buyer who is strictly money oriented will be turned off. In other words, a buyer may want to purchase the property, but may not want the bonus. The buyer may not want a cruise or need a car or TV. When that buyer sees what you're offering, they may simply turn away because they're not interested.

Don't worry about this. Remember, at least half of the purpose behind a bonus giveaway is just to draw attention to your prop-erty. If it simply gets buyers to come and look, it has served a great purpose.

On the other hand, if a buyer who might not otherwise have considered your property comes and looks, and wants to buy, but, as it turns out, isn't interested in your bonus, don't worry. The essence of real estate is negotiating. The buyer shouldn't walk away just because you're offering a bonus without at least at-tempting to negotiate with you.

For example, such a buyer might ask, "If I were to make an offer, would you reduce your price by the cost of the bonus giveaway?"

Answer yes, of course you would. Don't limit your answer by saying something such as, "Of course, the bonus costs a lot less than you probably think." Never mind that your cost is low. Let the buyer think the giveaway is a big thing, a big bonus.

What you want is that offer. There's nothing to negotiate until the buyer commits to making an offer. But once he or she puts up earnest money (a cash deposit—never consider any offer that isn't accompanied by it) everything becomes negotiable. Now you can bring up the fact that the $10,000 cruise is really only costing you

$3,500, and that's all you can come down. Or the car really only will cost $6,500, and here's the dealer's invoice to prove it.

A bonus giveaway shouldn't limit you. It will suck in more buyers and actually give you more negotiating room than less.

There are, then, seven good reasons to use giveaways. Above we've couched them in terms of common misconceptions. Here they are written plainly:

Reasons to Use Giveaways

1. It generates interest.
2. You aren't the only one doing it.
3. It isn't expensive.
4. You can't afford not to in a down market.
5. You don't need cash.
6. It shouldn't reduce the money you receive for a sale, but may increase the price and reduce the time spent.
7. It will increase the number of potential buyers.

Don't Hide It

Having thus considered the reasons for using giveaways, let's just spend a moment on marketing. A giveaway is a great marketing tool. It's something you have that many people want. It's also something many sellers aren't offering.

Therefore, you want to do everything possible to let potential buyers know about it. If you have your home listed with an agent, don't keep it a secret from the agent, and make sure he or she doesn't hide it from other agents. If your property is already listed, have your agent send out a special bulletin announcing the bonus. Have them talk it up at sales meetings in the office, with other offices, and at weekly or monthly real estate board meetings (when brokers from the entire area come by).

If there are advertisements by you or your broker, mention the giveaway prominently in them. You'll be surprised by the number of responses when your newspaper ad mentions there's a car or a cruise going with the house.

Put it on the sign in front. Two simple words will do, such as, "Car Bonus" or "Cruise Bonus." Don't worry about buyers missing it. They are very clever at picking out any advantage to them, and if they see this as an advantage, you can be sure they'll pounce on it and, if nothing else, ask you or your agent to explain.

In short, if you're going to use a promotional giveaway, get the most out of it you can by advertising it in every way you can.

Pitfalls of Promotional Giveaways

Thus far we've been treating the promotional giveaway as if it were a panacea. It's not. There are some drawbacks to it that need to be considered.

First, keep in mind that throwing in a promotional giveaway won't help you overcome intrinsic drawbacks to your property. If you're in a bad location, offering a free cruise won't convince the buyer your location is any better. If the house is a mess and is rundown, a free TV won't convince the buyer it really is in better shape than it looks. If it needs paint and the landscaping is shot, offering a free cruise may actually work against you by making the buyer think you don't want him to get near the house too soon!

The giveaway is what it's been called in this chapter, a bonus. It's purpose is to increase interest in your property and to compel buyers to dream a little bit. But if your property is a nightmare, their dreams won't help. In short, you can't expect a bonus to take the place of paint, cleaning, and landscaping.

Second, a bonus isn't going to get you last year's price. It may help you to get a better price than you might otherwise expect.

But, it won't return you to recent peak prices. Nobody is going to pay $50,000 more for your property because you're throwing in a $10,000 Buick.

Finally, there's the matter of your own frustration at having to offer a bonus at all. We'll touch on the subject of sales exhaustion later in this book, but it bears mentioning here.

Typically a seller won't offer a promotional giveaway until the last resort. Only when nothing else works will most sellers be likely to think about the bonus.

However, by this time the seller has probably been through quite a few hurdles. He may have spent months keeping his property clean and neat for buyers who seldom come by, and when they do come, are uninterested. He may be shelling out money for a mortgage payment he can't really afford. He may already have found a new house that he wants and can't get into until his current one sells.

All of this frustration may come to a head when he finally does decide on offering a promotional bonus. It usually takes a form something like, "Here I am having to baby this house, make payments, be inconvenienced, and now, on top of it all, I'm giving the buyers a bonus. Enough is enough. I not taking any more!"

As noted earlier, the frustration may be justified, but it's not helpful. It won't get his house sold. In fact, it may keep it from getting sold.

If you're experiencing frustration with selling, take a break, perhaps a weekend off. Then come back fully prepared to try again as if you were starting off for the first time. Don't dwell on the advantages buyers have over you the seller. (Remember, as soon as you sell, you too can be a buyer!) Just consider it another technique in your armory of sales tools. Don't let sales exhaustion defeat your use of a promotional giveaway. You'll only be hurting yourself if you do.

Promotional Giveaway Ideas

Here are some suggestions of items you may want to consider as giveaways. The list is by no means complete. Often the more creative the idea, the better.

    Car
    Cruise
    Big Screen TV
    Stereo System
    Weekend at a Resort
    Spa
    Membership at a Local Gym
    Gardening/Pool/Maid Service for a Year
    Six Months' Gasoline for Buyer's Car
    All Utilities Paid for Six Months
    Mortgage Payments Paid for Six Months
    Two Years' Taxes Paid
    Ten Years' Home Warranty Paid

(The list, of course, is limited only by your imagination.)

7

Saving on the Commission

In the past I've always advocated using a real estate agent to help sell your home. The reason is simple: The agent is set up to deal with buyers, to handle the paper work, and to merchandise your property.

However, in a very down market things are somewhat different. Here, with few buyers around, and with those who want to buy looking strictly for bargains, you may actually be better off, in some situations, selling on your own. In this chapter we'll look at how you can save the commission and increase the chances for a sale. (Also check into chapter three for additional insights.)

When to Try Selling on Your Own

Normally the fastest and most efficient way to sell your home for the highest price is to use the services of a real estate agent. Nearly all agents are members of a Multiple Listing Service, and when you list with one, they normally agree to "cobroke," or share the listing with all the others in the area. Thus, by listing you may actually be acquiring the services of hundreds if not thousands of agents.

Of course, as we saw earlier, it takes a sharp agent to spread the word about the selling features of your house and to get the other agents interested. Nevertheless, the best way, initially, to market your house is with an agent. (In the past, I've advocated taking a period of time, say a month, to try to sell by yourself. If you can't, then go with the agent.)

But, what do you do when you've listed your house for the normal three month period and, because of a down market, the agent can't sell it? Or, what's actually happened to many sellers, the home has been listed for six months or even a year and still there is no buyer. Do you just keep relisting it? Do you sell it yourself?

My feeling is that if you've given agents a chance and they haven't been able to sell your house, then it's time to try something else. But what else is there?

Low Commission Agents

The first alternative I would suggest is a low commission agent. Here you get the benefits of having your house placed on the Multiple Listing Service and an agent's sign, but you also can sell on your own and not be liable for a commission.

Perhaps a word about commissions is in order. When you list with an agent, you sign a listing agreement. This agreement spells out the commission and how and when it's to be paid. Typically, a full-service agent wants an "Exclusive Right To Sell" listing. When you sign this it means the agent gets the commission no matter who sells your house during the listing period, even if you sell it yourself!

While many sellers are at first aghast at this, it actually makes a lot of sense. Some buyers and sellers are unscrupulous. If it were not for this type of agreement, the agent might find a buyer, who then might get together with the seller and work out a separate deal (to avoid paying a commission). It's understandable that agents are unwilling to give full service to a seller and a house without the kind of protection this listing offers. In fact, my advice to you is that if you plan to list with a full-service agent, you give them a Right To Sell listing.

(For hints on dealing with listings, I suggest *Tips And Traps When Selling Your Home,* McGraw-Hill, 1990.)

However, here we're not talking about a full service agent. (Presumably you've already tried that and it didn't work out.) Instead, here we're talking about an agent who will provide limited services for a low fee. Just what service will this agent provide and for how much?

Services Offered

The services offered by these agents vary. They may include any or all of the following:

Services of a Low Commission Agent

1. Agent's sign and phone number in front of house.
2. Help with all the paper work.
3. Showing the house to prospective buyers the agent produces.
4. Listing on the Multiple Listing Service so other agents can collect a commission.
5. Open Houses.
6. Help securing financing for the buyer.
7. Advertising.

In short, it would appear on the surface that a low commission agent provides everything a full-service agent offers. That's not really so.

Typically in this sort of arrangement, you will have to pay for any advertising of the property. Further, for an open house, the agent will provide the signs, but will not be there. You have to sit at the house trying to hook buyers.

As for help with financing, unless the agent is a mortgage broker and is receiving a separate financing fee, the help usually consists of a list of lenders, the current rates they are charging, and a hearty "Good luck!" to the buyer.

Yes, the agent may list the property on the Multiple Listing Service, but don't expect him to spend a lot of time, energy, or money talking it up to other agents. And don't expect a lot of other agents to be thrilled to show your house.

In short, with a low commission agent you can expect to get the flavor of a full-service real estate agent without the meat and bones. Of course, you're getting what you pay for.

Your Costs

Your costs for a low commission agent vary. While the going rate for commissions in the area might be 6 or 7 percent, they may ask for 2 or 3. Typically, however, there is a catch. If they sell the house, you may only pay 3 percent. However, if you want them to list it on the Multiple Listing Service and another broker sells, then you probably will be liable for the entire 6 percent, 3 to them and 3 to the other broker.

Note: As mentioned earlier, it's important to understand that the commission rate is not set by anyone except you and the agent through negotiation. Neither the local real estate board, the National Organization of Realtors, nor any other group sets a rate of commission. However, some brokers simply will not work for less than a set rate. If that's the case, you may have to pay their fee or look elsewhere.

Sellers are often thrilled to sign up for the lower rate of commission. After all, if your house is selling for $150,000, each 1 percent of commission that you save is another $1,500 in your pocket. This trend toward paying half a commission may be part of a bigger trend toward a separation between buyer's brokers and seller's brokers. As a seller you pay half a fee to your broker and the buyer pays half a fee to his. This separation really makes a lot of sense, and it encourages better fiduciary relationships all around.

A Fixed Fee Agent

Another recent trend is to use a fixed fee agent. With a fixed fee agent, you agree to pay the agent up front a certain fee for listing your house. Usually this fee is under $500. You also agree to sign an Exclusive Agency agreement. (Remember, this means you pay no commission if you sell the property yourself.)

Here's how it all works. For the fee, the agent places your property on the Multiple Listing Service and puts a sign out front. He also agrees to help you fill out a sales agreement if you find a buyer on your own. Finally, he agrees to minimally look for buyers. In other words, if a buyer comes by his office and asks to see your house, he'll show it.

There is also a commission structure. Again, this varies enormously from agent to agent. But the way it usually works is that if an agent from another office cobrokes a deal and brings you a buyer, whose offer you accept, you will end up paying a full commission, say 6 percent. If, however, the agent with whom you listed finds a buyer without having to cobroke it, you only have to pay half a commission, say 3 percent. In both cases the up-front money (around $500) is deducted from the commission.

On the other hand, if you sell the property yourself, you've only paid the roughly $500 fee. You owe no commission. If this sounds a bit confusing, let's try taking it one step at a time.

If the Agent Sells the Property

1. The full commission if a different office cobrokes the deal.
2. Half the usual commission if he sells it himself.
3. The up-front fee is normally deducted from both

commissions above in the event of the agent finding a buyer.

If You Sell the Property Yourself

1. No commission at all.
2. Only the up-front fee (usually under $500).

If the Property Doesn't Sell

1. You only pay the up-front fee.

Of course, the big question is, does it work?

The answer is, yes, a surprisingly large number of times. Quite frankly, when I first heard of the above arrangement, I was skeptical. Having been in real estate for twenty-nine years, I was used to the traditional brokerage fee for a full-service agent. I felt the cut rate fees of low-service agents only did a disservice to the seller.

However, having been exposed to a number of agents who have successfully used the above system, as well as to sellers who have successfully sold this way, I am happy to report it is an idea whose time may be soon at hand. You can indeed do well selling your house this way.

Understanding the Strategy

Before you rush out to list with a low commission broker, however, it's important to be sure you fully understand the strategy behind the above arrangement. It's actually a modified way for you to sell your house by yourself. The only advantage comes from your being willing to spend the time, effort, and sometimes money to look for buyers yourself.

Actually, in the deals I've seen in the current down market made using low commission brokers, the seller finds the buyer a surprisingly large number of times. In short, its best use is probably for those who really want to sell their houses themselves.

In other words, you want the best of both worlds. You want your house listed on the Multiple Listing Service so brokers can work on it and bring you any buyers they may have. However, you also want to work on selling it yourself and not have to pay a commission if you are successful. If this is your situation, then a low commission listing may be ideal for you.

Note: It's important to understand we're not talking about trying to get a full-service agent to work for less. Some sellers make the mistake of thinking they can have it all. They want full service, but they also don't want to pay. Typically they will offer a full-service agent an Exclusive Agency agreement thinking they will get the agent's full-time efforts, yet they can sell the property themselves without paying a commission.

No full-service agent worth his salt will work under such an arrangement. Many, if they are scrupulously ethical, will simply turn down your listings. Others may take and file it away doing nothing for you.

If you want to get a low commission broker, you have to look for one who specializes in this area. Typically they advertise their reduced fees in the yellow pages of your phone book.

Selling by Owner

As noted above, the real advantage of using a low commission agent comes about when you really think you have a shot at selling the house yourself. But, at the same time you want to keep your options open by having your house listed. It's a way to keep one foot in each camp.

However, you may be of a more independent nature. You may feel that you will take charge and sell your property by owner. (In the trade the term is "FSBO"—For Sale By Owner.)

As I noted earlier, in a normal market I advise against trying to sell entirely by yourself. Agents are set up to handle sales, you are not. In a normal market you might as well try flying a commercial jet (instead of being a passenger) as sell your own home.

But what if, as also noted earlier, you've tried it with an agent, or even several agents? It has been six months to a year and your house simply has not sold. Isn't it now time to go a different direction? Isn't it now time to try selling by yourself?

Advantages of Selling by Owner in a Down Market

The down market conditions actually do provide you with certain advantages when you sell by owner which do not exist in a normal market. They include the following:

1. More buyer appeal.
2. Greater flexibility with price.
3. The ability to work more closely with a buyer on terms.

Let's consider each separately.

More Buyer Appeal

In a down market, buyers are looking for bargains. If truth be told, most buyers won't make an offer on a property unless they are convinced there is some sort of bargain there for them, even if they otherwise like the house and would choose to live there! When you sell by owner, you hold up the allure of a bargain.

For some reason, buyers tend to feel that a house that's offered outside of the normal real estate market, that is, that's not listed, might be a bargain. Put up a "For Sale By Owner" sign in your yard and you can expect to get a lot of traffic through. (Unfortunately, much of that traffic will be real estate agents trying to get a listing. But buyers should be there, too.)

It's now up to you to take advantage of the additional traffic. As noted earlier, you'll have to approach each buyer with a combination of techniques. On the one hand, you'll try to convince them to love the house, so they'll make an offer. On the other, you'll attempt to give them a good deal, so they'll make an offer.

The bottom line, however, is that buyers will see your house as having a certain allure simply because you're selling by owner. They will stop by, and if you play your cards right, they may make an offer.

Warning! Don't be pushy. Buyers expect a seller who isn't using an agent to be knowledgeable and reasonable. But they are deathly afraid of desperate sellers who want to sell so badly that they try to push the house onto the buyer. You can't *make* anyone buy your house. They have to decide they want it on their own.

Greater Flexibility with Price

In an earlier chapter we talked about sellers who couldn't find buyers when their houses were listed because they were asking unrealistic prices. Therefore, these sellers then chose to attempt to sell by owner, unfortunately at the same unrealistic prices. Consequently, they still couldn't sell.

However, if you are willing to ask a realistic price, then you do stand a good chance of finding a buyer. When you sell by owner, you have greater flexibility in pricing. For example, let's say your house is selling for $200,000. When you list, you might end up paying a 6 percent commission, or $12,000. Your net after commission would only be $188,000.

Now, you can offer the house at $188,000 and still get the same net. In short you can pass the commission on to the buyer.

Note: This is a real advantage only if your home is realistically priced. If your house was worth $200,000 three years ago but the current market price is $150,000, knocking off a $12,000 commission will still leave you $38,000 above market. You're not likely to attract buyers there.

On the other hand, if $200,000 is the current market price, then knocking 6 percent or $12,000 off could make a big difference to buyers, and could get you a sale.

Warning! Don't try to save the commission for yourself. This is not a normal market, it's a down market, and you need every advantage you can get. If you try to sell by owner, in the above example, for the full $200,000 hoping to pocket the commission yourself, you'll likely end up not selling. The advantage you hope to gain from selling by owner is offering the buyer a lower price coming directly from your savings on the commission. It's a foolish seller who blows a sale by trying to save a few bucks off the commission.

The Ability to Work More Closely with a Buyer on Terms

When you deal through an agent, you deal with the buyer at some distance. Often, in fact, the only time you see the buyer is when he or she walks through the house when first looking at it and then at a final "walk through" just before closing.

This can actually be an advantage in many cases, particularly if there's hard negotiating to be done and the buyer is adversarial. However, in other cases, the buyer is something akin to a friend.

This is particularly the case when the buyers fall in love with your house. If that happens, the buyers may want to see a lot of you, to ask if you'll leave the rug in the hall or if you'll sell them the cute little porcelain duck you have placed in the garden.

Being in a direct relationship with buyers here can help. The buyers will feel free to discuss their needs and concerns with you, and you'll be more directly aware of what they want and what progress they're making in putting together the money needed to close the deal. If the buyers are having some sort of problem financially, say in raising the down payment, you may be willing to help out in terms of a second mortgage or other seller financing. (If you hadn't established a relationship with them through direct dealings, you might be more hesitant to do this and could, conceivably, lose a deal because of it.)

In short, by selling yourself, you have the opportunity to work more closely with the buyers and will feel more comfortable in manipulating the terms to meet their needs.

Disadvantages of Selling by Owner, and Overcoming Them

On the other hand, there are distinct disadvantages you face selling by owner in a down market. Let's consider these:

You can't work full time at selling.

You can only sell your home part time. An agent, on the other hand, is at work on it full-time. Further, by listing your property on the Multiple Listing Service, all the agents in your area (probably hundreds) can also help sell your property.

The answer here is that the agent has hundreds, perhaps thousands of homes to sell. You only have one. You may feel that working part time on one house is better than having a lot of agents work full time on a very great number of houses.

You're not experienced in real estate transactions.

This is often the biggest stumbling block for many sellers. Yes, you know the sales agreement is a legally binding document and has to be drawn just right. But, you may not know how to get it drawn. Are you going to be stymied just because you don't possess the technical knowledge to handle the paper work?

You shouldn't. There are ways around it, one being to obtain the services of a helper agent. In a down market it should be little trouble to get an agent who will agree to take care of the paper-work for you. They will draw up the sales agreement and do any other items that might be required.

Because of the liability involved, however, an agent in a normal market will either be hesitant to do this or will ask for a sizeable amount of money, say a thousand dollars or more. In today's market, however, availability should be easier and price should be much lower.

As an alternative, you might want to get the services of a real estate lawyer. Presumably (but not always) you will be assured that the agreement will be more legally binding. Since you may want the services of an attorney anyhow as you proceed through the deal, this may be a good bet. But be prepared to pay upwards of $500 for the attorney's services. And be sure to look for an attorney who specializes in real estate. Just because someone has passed the bar doesn't mean they know the ins and outs of real estate transactions.

How to Show Your House

Finally, there's the matter of showing the property when you sell by owner. We touched on this earlier, but it warrants a special section.

There is an art to showing a house. Many real estate agents acquire it immediately. Others take years to learn it. Many others never do. If you're going to sell by owner, you need to have at least the rudiments of an understanding of how it's done. Here we are going to look at just a couple of basic approaches.

First, it's important to remember that when you're showing a house to a buyer, it's like selling anything else, from tires to shoes. What you are really selling is yourself. If the buyer likes you, chances are they will like the house. On the other hand, if the buyer doesn't think you're so wonderful, don't expect them to be too thrilled about the house, either.

My suggestion, therefore, is to be as personable with any prospective buyers as possible. Engage them in conversation, and get to know them. Don't think of them as buyers, but instead as people who are going to become long-term and highly regarded friends. In fact, one method some successful salespeople use to help them in their business is to visualize the word "Friend" right on the face of their client.

With a buyer, you simply want to show them what you have to offer and then get an answer. With a friend, however, you want to find out what it is they really need and then see if you can satisfy that need. If you can, then you should be able to make a sale. If you can't, then it really doesn't make much difference what you say . . . they'll look elsewhere.

Next, it's important to remember that no matter how much buyers may or may not know about houses and real estate, they know a great deal about people. And they can instantly sense when someone is trying to manipulate them. Let me give you an example.

A buyer walks into your house and you begin talking to her. She lets you know she is looking for a home with an all electric kitchen. Your house has a gas burning oven and stove. You've hit a snag. What do you do?

Some sellers begin telling the buyers why it's really better for them to have gas than electricity. Perhaps it costs less, doesn't break down as often, and works better. The seller may be very sincere about this. But the buyer is no fool. She looks around and realizes the seller only has gas to offer. Consequently, everything the seller says becomes suspect. The buyer begins to think the seller is saying this just to get the sale. This produces mistrust. The buyer begins to feel manipulated. Suddenly there are lots of other things wrong with your house. And a potential sale is lost.

The mistake here is that the seller attempted to manipulate the buyer, to change the buyer's wants. The seller didn't have what the buyer wanted, so the seller attempted to get the buyer to want something else. Some very good salespeople can sometimes do this, but usually not very often.

Perhaps a better course of action might have been to agree with the buyer and then suggest that if the buyer really wanted electricity, you would put it in. An electric range and oven cost under $400, and running the electrical cable, depending on how your house was originally wired, may be only a couple of hundred more. (If your house is older and wasn't originally wired for 220 volts, on the other hand, it could be far more expensive.) Isn't it worth the money to get a sale in a down market?

Of course, you don't have to sound enthusiastic about it. But you can leave it open for the buyer. They want electricity, you'll be willing to consider putting it in and throwing in a new stove and oven to boot. Now that might be just enough to get someone to make an offer. In any event, they will certainly think you're being straightforward and non-manipulative.

Of course, keep in mind that you might never need to go through the hassle. Once you've eliminated the stumbling block, you can move on. Perhaps the buyers on their own will decide they really can live with gas and would rather have you knock down the price a bit (something which you undoubtedly knew you were going to have to do, anyway) than put in a new oven and stove.

The whole point here is that unless you're a super good salesperson, the best advice is to be totally honest at all times with prospective buyers. Don't try to change their wants. Don't try to manipulate them. If there's something they must have that your house lacks, see if you can't put it in.

Finally, and perhaps most importantly, allow potential buyers to fall in love with your home. Yes, you can show buyers your favorite features. But, allow them time to discover features they like about your home on their own. Perhaps the best time spent can be when you leave the buyers alone to ponder the house while you make an excuse to do this or that somewhere else.

Of course, there's a lot more to selling than the small amount we've covered here. But if you keep these three concepts in mind—think of buyers as friends, be totally honest, and give them room to acquire a feeling of ownership—you'll be a lot closer to a sale.

The Bottom Line

Overcoming Those Reasons

It is possible to save the cost of a commission, typically between 5 and 7 percent of the sales price. That's a fair chunk of money. And in today's down market, since you're probably going to take less than you want anyway, saving that would make a big difference.

Of course, it could mean putting in a lot more work yourself. Even if you sell with a lower cost broker, you'll still have to come forward with some extra effort. You may have to put yourself out on weekends, take your chances with buyers who come by. You may have to seek out a real estate attorney or a lower cost broker. And there's always the unforeseen hassle.

However, if you end up saving a commission, it all could indeed be worth it.

8

5 Ways Out: Trade Up, Lease Option, Package, Partnership, Time-Sharing

Thus far we've discussed fairly superficial things you can do, such as promotional items and cosmetic improvements, that will help you to sell your home. Now we're going to move on to some very specific plans for getting out of your house. Some of these are well known and used frequently by people who need desperately to sell. Others may be new to you. You will want to read each over carefully to see if it might apply to your situation.

The Trade Up

The trade up is based on the assumption that you will want to buy a new home once you get out of your present one. If you don't want to get into a new home, forget about the trade up—it probably isn't for you. (You will, however, want to move on to some of the other suggestions in this chapter.)

In the first chapter we talked about selling at a low price but offsetting that sale by buying at an equally low price. Here we're going to do something similar. However, instead of buying and selling, we're going to work out a trade. And instead of dealing with another individual who wants to sell his home, we're going to work with a builder.

The Builder's Perspective

In order to understand how and why this scenario could work, it's first important to glimpse the market from the perspective of builders. Most of the larger builder/developers work speculatively. That is, they put up houses without having firm commitments to purchase from buyers. They might build a tract of fifty homes without a single confirmed sale. They hope that by the time the houses are completed or, at least shortly thereafter, buyers will come along and make purchases. This is in the great American tradition of home building.

In normal markets it usually works out well. The builder puts up a few models and has a sales staff to take orders. Buyers come by and make purchases during the construction phase. In a well run development, the builder will have a steady flow of cash coming in. Initially he will have money from construction loans from banks or savings and loan institutions. Then, as he completes his first homes and sells them, buyers will be bringing him money, which he'll use to pay off the existing construction loans and to help finance the next phase of the tract. (This is why builders typically put tracts up in phases instead of all at once.) Eventually, by the time the last homes are built, the majority of the first homes are already sold, and people are already living in them.

Of course, this is the ideal. But in a normal market, it usually works out pretty close, if the builder is any good. In a down market, however, it can turn into a disaster.

Builder Troubles in a Down Market

Problems occur when real estate goes into a recession. Then the anticipated buyers don't show up, and this puts the builder in a desperate situation. Houses keep going up, but they don't get sold, and the cash flow dries up.

The builder continues to have to pay interest on the construction loans for homes already built or under construction, but there's little to no money coming in from buyers. As a result, the builder will begin dipping into his savings to keep the project alive and out of foreclosure. He will also cancel phases that have not been started. However, work that's already begun is almost impossible to cancel—once he begins drawing down on his construction loan the interest starts to run, and the only good way out is to sell the property and pay off that loan. If he can't find a buyer and can't keep making the interest payments, he goes broke.

Such are the risks of speculative building. This is why the National Association of Home Builders predicts under a million new homes will be built in 1991, down from close to two million only a few years earlier, and a sixteen-year low.

Why Build at All?

I'm sure some readers are wondering why any new houses are being built speculatively at all. In a down market, why would any builders take the chance?

This is an important question because it addresses the nature of home construction in this country. The only way builders make money is to build. When they aren't building, they are literally out of business. With no new homes going up there's no money coming in from construction loans. Without buyers for their homes, there's no money coming in from sales. In short, unless they build, there's no money coming in at all.

Of course, they could always go into another trade. They might become barbers or politicians. But, if they want to stay builders, they have to keep on building. Thus, no matter how bad the market gets, there are always some builders, usually those with the deepest pockets and the greatest resources, who continue to struggle along. Typically these are the eternal optimists who hope that by the time they get their houses done, the market will have turned around and they can then sell for a big profit.

This, then, is the builder's perspective. In a strong market, it makes very good sense. It wasn't all that long ago that buyers were lining up to purchase new homes. Builders were able to raise their prices at each new phase without significantly increasing their costs. It was one of the great gravy trains of all time, as far as making money is concerned.

In a bad market, however, it's quite something else, and that's where you come in.

Taking Advantage of the Builder's Dilemma

The builder's greatest foe is time. He must get those houses up and sold before the interest on the construction loans eats him up. When the market turns sour and his houses sit there unsold, he gets desperate and looks for any kind of reasonable way out. You can offer him that way out.

The key is to offer to take away those deadly construction loan interest payments. You do that by getting a "take-out" or permanent loan on the house, and making the payments yourself. In other words, you take over ownership and get a new mortgage.

The builder will be thrilled to have you do this. However, there are two unresolved issues. The first is the builder's equity in his new home. Presumably he hoped to sell the house for substantially more than the construction loan. That equity represents some of his initial seed money as well as his anticipated profits. Unless he is at the brink of foreclosure, he is going to want to recoup some of that.

Second, there's the matter of your own house. Most likely you can't make the payments both on your own house and on the builder's. For most people, it's hard enough to make one mortgage payment, let alone two.

These two problems, sometimes, can cancel each other out. The way is simply this: You trade houses with the builder—he gets your house, and you get his.

The benefits for you should be obvious. You end up with a

brand new house, your ultimate goal. And you get rid of your old house, your short term goal.

Why the Builder Would Go for It

The benefits for the builder are also there, but are not quite so obvious. He gets rid of his construction loan and interest payments. And he converts his equity into your home.

But, he still has the mortgage on your property (most likely a new mortgage since the old one may not be assumable). And he still has payments.

However, and this is the real crux of the plan, he may be able to rent out your house for close to his mortgage payments, which he couldn't do on a more expensive new home. In other words, he converts his equity into a long-term rental.

The Key to the Plan

In order to make this whole scheme work, your house has to have two key features. First, it must be a suitable rental property. That means it must be in an area where it can be rented fairly easily for a fairly high price.

Second, you must have a lot of equity in it, and, generally speaking, your sales price must be lower than the price of the new home.

The reason this works is that rental income can often come close to meeting payments on lower priced properties, but rarely can do so on higher priced ones. Let's consider an example:

Trade Up Example

You own a home which you are trying to sell for $250,000 and on which you owe $100,000. Your equity in your home is $150,000 (forgetting costs of sale, for the moment):

Your asking price	$ 250,000
Mortgage	100,000
Equity	150,000

The builder has a home which he is trying to sell for $350,000 on which he has a construction loan of $180,000. His equity is $170,000.

Builder's asking price	$ 350,000
Construction loan	180,000
Equity	170,000

You trade the builder for his property at full price and get a new mortgage for $200,000. You have now successfully converted your equity into a new home. The builder has also received some cash ($20,000) from the loan you obtained.

Your equity	$ 150,000
New mortgage	200,000
Your purchase price	350,000

At the same time the builder takes over your property, which now has a fairly low mortgage on it, and rents it out.

Builder's new equity	$ 130,000
New mortgage on your old house (from which the builder receives $20,000 in cash; remember your old loan was only $100,000.)	120,000
Builder's purchase price	250,000

If you have trouble grasping the concept here, just remember that what's happening is that you're trading up. You're moving from a $250,000 house to a $350,000 house and getting a bigger mortgage with bigger payments. The builder, on the other hand, is moving down. He's dropping from a $350,000 house down to a $250,000 house, and moving from a construction loan of $180,000 to a new lower payment mortgage of $120,000. He's getting some cash out (a total of $40,000 in this example), but more important, his payments on the mortgage will be lower, allowing him to come close to breaking even on a rental.

You're doing it because your goal is to move up to a new house, and this is a way to achieve that goal in a market where you can't sell your present home. The builder's doing it because his goal is to get out from under the interest payments on his construction loan and into a lower cost house, which he can rent until the market turns around. Then, he can resell it and recoup his equity.

Will this Really Work?

Sometimes. It depends on the circumstances, but when they are right, it can work well. The trade up is a realistic option that can get you out of your present home and into a new one of your dreams in a down market. But, as with all deals, there are pitfalls.

There are a number of problems with the trade up, and we'll cover a few of them here.

Pitfall #1—Your property or the builder's isn't suited to the trade.

Both you and the builder may wish to move forward on this deal. But as noted, the situation must be right. You must have a lot of equity in a lower priced home and must be willing and able to get a higher mortgage. The builder must be desperate to get out and be willing to put his equity into a house he can rent until the market turns around.

If these conditions are not right, the deal will not work. If your house is too expensive or your equity too small (and your mortgage too high), it might not be rentable for close to payments, and the builder won't be interested.

Pitfall #2—Tax consequences.

Every real estate transaction has tax consequences of one sort or another, and this deal is no exception. For the purpose of our example, we've ignored taxes. However, if you're selling for more than you paid, you will probably have a capital gain. (An exception would be if you had spent a lot of money improving your old home.) If you have to pay tax on the sale, you will lose a lot of your equity.

However, as we noted in an earlier chapter, if your old house was your personal residence and the new home is likewise your personal residence, you may be able to defer or "roll over" that gain and not pay any taxes at the time of the transaction.

It depends on how the deal is structured. You may (or may not) be required to "sell" your old house to the builder and then "buy" the new one from him as two separate transactions in order to meet the deferral requirements. You should definitely consult with your CPA or tax attorney to be sure you don't do something to your disadvantage.

There are similar problems for the builder. He may need a tax deferred trade—Section 1031 trade of like-kind properties—in order to avoid paying taxes on his end. Again, each deal will be different, and it might be that the different tax needs will preclude you and the builder from completing the transaction. On the other hand, one or the other of you may be willing to compromise to make the deal. The tax complexities should not be underestimated and should be carefully weighed and analyzed by a competent CPA or tax attorney before moving forward with the deal.

Pitfall #3—The builder can't get a new mortgage on your home.

In order for this deal to work, typically you will need to get a new mortgage on the new home (to pay off the construction loan and possibly get the builder back some equity), and the builder may need to get a new mortgage on your property. We're presuming you can qualify and obtain a new mortgage. You may not be able to do that, but if you're looking to buy a newer and more expensive home, I'm assuming you will.

In some cases, however, the builder will have trouble getting a new mortgage on your old house. The reason is that it's easier by far to get a mortgage on a property in which you intend to live than on one you intend to rent out, especially in a down market. Further, the builder's credit may already be stretched thin—he may simply not qualify. Your chances of finding a builder who's so desperate that he will consider trading down and at the same time so solvent that he has no trouble qualifying for a new mortgage are not always good. (There are lenders who will lend simply on the basis of the property's value without regard to the ability of the borrower to repay. But these charge a higher interest rate, which the builder may not want.)

Any deal you sign with the builder should be contingent upon his being able to qualify for and obtain a new mortgage on your property within a reasonable amount of time. No new loan, possibly no deal.

Warning! The builder may want to keep the original mortgage on your old property. The builder may come to you and say something like, "Listen, I'm having trouble getting a new loan on your house. Why don't we simply keep the existing mortgage? After all, I only intend to rent the house out until the market turns around. Once it does, I'll sell the house and everything will work out fine."

There are serious legal problems here. Most modern mortgages (unless they are FHA insured or VA guaranteed, and even here there could be some difficulties) are *not* fully assumable. That means the buyer can't take over your old loan without at least doing some minimal qualifying, which in this case the builder, presumably, couldn't do.

Being not assumable means that as soon as you sell or trade your property, the mortgage is called and has to be paid off in full. When the builder suggests keeping the original mortgage, what he may be suggesting is that you not tell the mortgage company he has taken over ownership of your property. This might lead to a lot of serious consequences for you, depending on how the deal is structured.

The way this kind of deal is usually structured is in the form of a "modified wraparound." Instead of you giving the builder a deed to the property, the recording of which would alert your present mortgage lender that the house was sold, you sign an agreement to sell (which is not recorded) and give the builder a mortgage for the entire value of the home, in the case of our example, $250,000. The new mortgage wraps around the old. Of course, there are no payments and no interest. When it's recorded, it looks like a second mortgage, and the lender of the first isn't alerted to a possible sale. The builder continues to make the payments on the first, which remains in your name. Eventually, when he sells the property, he pays off the mortgage, and you give a deed to the new buyers.

There are lots of problems here. The first is that if the builder doesn't make the payments on your original mortgage, the lender is going to come after you, not him. You might have to make the payments yourself in order to protect your credit, yet because of the way the deal is structured, you might not be able to recoup that money from the builder.

Second, the fact that there is no recorded sale would prevent you from tax deferring your gain in a roll over. The builder might argue that it's only a matter of time until there is a sale. But, if you move to a new residence and the old residence is rented (which the builder plans to do), and the sale doesn't occur within certain time limits determined by the Internal Revenue Service, the deal might not qualify for the deferral of gain on the sale of a personal residence, possibly resulting in serious tax consequences for you.

In short, going along with a request to keep the old non-assumable mortgage on the sly is asking for trouble. If you're shrewd, and you or your real estate lawyer structure the deal well, yes, you might pull it off. On the other hand, it might end up costing you more money than if you had simply forgotten about the builder and hung onto your house until a legitimate buyer came along.

My advice is that if the builder says the only way he can make the deal is by faking the sale and tricking the existing lender, you pass on it.

Why Doesn't the Builder Simply Rent Out His New Home Instead of Buying Yours?

This is a final question which some readers, I am sure, are asking. Instead of going to all the hassle of trading down to your home, why doesn't the builder simply rent out his new home?

There are several reasons. First off, once it's rented it's no longer new and no longer commands a new home's price.

Second, most new homes cost too much. Rarely can they be rented for even half of the mortgage payments. It's only by getting an older home with a lower mortgage that the builder can hope to break even.

Third and finally, the builder can't keep the construction loan on the property forever. The construction loan is typically issued for under three years, sometimes under twelve months. Once the house is built and all the money withdrawn, it must be paid off in full. To do this, a "take-out" or permanent loan must be arranged. Many times the builder, in a down market, cannot qualify for the take-out loan on the same property for which he qualified for the original construction loan! Therefore, he must quickly sell or trade in order to avoid losing everything to the bank in foreclosure. (In actual practice, the lender will often work with the builder, extending the time he needs to find a buyer. But the extensions don't go on forever, and the interest never stops running.)

Lease Option

The second way out we'll consider is the lease option. This is a technique that does not sell your house or rent it, but achieves a kind of middle ground. In a down market where you have to move, it may be a very good option for you, particularly when combined with a refinance.

Understanding a Lease Option

To grasp the concept, it's necessary first to be sure we're clear on what a lease and an option are.

The Lease

A lease is a contract to rent your house to someone over a set period of time. Many leases are written for one year. Often the lessee or tenant pays the first and last month's rent up front as well as a security deposit. This is opposed to month-to-month tenancy, where the tenant can move out with only thirty days' notice. Under a lease, the tenant agrees to stay for the entire term of the lease. (Of course, if the tenant can't pay and moves out, there's really very little you can do, from a practical standpoint.)

The Option

An option, on the other hand, is an agreement to buy for a fixed price at a specified time in the future. If you are familiar with commodity or stock options, then you have a leg up on understanding real estate options.

In a real estate option the optionee agrees to purchase your property at a certain date in the future, usually from one to three years, for a price you agree upon today. (In some options, the price can be determined in the future according to a formula, for example, today's price plus an increase equal to the increase in the cost of living during the intervening time.)

Under the option, you are committed to sell at the future date (or before it) for the agreed upon price. However, the buyer has the *option* of passing on the deal or going forward with it. If he goes forward, he is said to be exercising his option.

For committing to sell, you are normally paid an option fee up front. It can be any amount.

To reiterate, in an option, you are committed to sell, but the buyer has the option of purchasing or not.

Combining a Lease and an Option

It works like this. You advertise for someone who wants to buy a home, but who doesn't have the down payment (a common enough occurrence in today's high priced market). Then you propose that they rent your house for a period of years (the lease).

A certain portion of each month's rent, however, will go toward the eventual purchase, which you guarantee to them at an agreed upon price (the option).

Be sure you understand what's being done here. The buyers are in reality tenants. However, typically they will pay a slightly higher rent, a portion of which will be set aside as their option money. (They may instead come up with this in cash when they move in.) If they decide to buy, that money will then be credited toward their down payment. If they decide not to buy, then it's lost like any other option money when the option isn't exercised.

The lease option increases your chances of finding buyer/ tenants because you're broadening the market. Perhaps someone wants to buy now and tie down today's low prices, but doesn't have the down payment. This offers them a way in. You will find there are far more people willing to consider a lease option in a down market than there are straight home buyers.

Advantages to You

If you want to get out in a down market and you can't sell outright, the lease option offers you certain plusses:

Plusses of the Lease Option

1. You can move out and know your house is rented for a fairly long period of time to tenants who will take good care of it (since they intend to buy it) and will make their monthly payments on time.

2. You have a built-in buyer for your house, if not immediately, then hopefully down the road.

3. The house is off your mind. In a lease option the tenant is often responsible for many of the small troubles that plague landlords, such as leaky faucets and broken windows.

On the other hand, it's not all advantages to you. There is a downside to a lease option which, I am sorry to say, many agents who promote them fail to mention:

Minuses of the Lease Option

1. Rarely does the option money received either from an increased amount of rent or as a lump sum payment equal the necessary down payment to qualify for a new mortgage on your home. That means that as the option runs out, the tenant/buyer has to come up with more money. For example, let's say your home is selling for $200,000 and the minimum necessary down payment is 10 percent or $20,000. You are crediting $200 of each month's rent for three years toward the purchase price (down payment). At the end of three years the tenant/buyers have paid in $7,600. But they still need an additional $12,400 to make the deal. If they don't have it now, they may not have it three years down the road and may not be able to complete the purchase.

2. Similarly, even if the tenant/buyers have the down payment, there's no guarantee they will be able to qualify for a new mortgage. You may find that you have no buyer at the end of the option period.

3. As the option term draws to a close, the tenant/ buyers may realize they can't buy, either because they don't have enough for the down payment or because they can't qualify. They may then object to making higher monthly payments, a portion of which goes to the option money, which they stand to lose if they don't buy. They may simply move out or, what's worse, stay and refuse to pay,

resulting in your having to go through a costly eviction. If they refuse to pay rent, you may have a more difficult time evicting them because they have greater rights than regular tenants.

Deciding Whether to Try It

The lease option works well typically for about the first half of the option time. For example, if the option is for three years, it usually works pretty well for the first eighteen months. Then, the tenant/buyer begins to realize they really won't be able to qualify or to come up with the down payment, and your troubles start.

How often do troubles start, and how often is the tenant/buyer able to exercise the option? There are no statistics kept (since it's done on an individual basis), but drawing on my own experience as well as that of many agents I deal with, I would say the tenant/buyers exercise their option perhaps 25 percent of the time and fail to do so 75 percent.

With such a high failure rate, why bother?

The answer is that even though the lease option may ultimately not work out, in the short run it can be a godsend, particularly if you have to get out right away. For example, you've got a job change and need to leave immediately. But, you can't until you do something about your house.

In a down market you can't sell. So, instead, you choose the lease option route. For the next eighteen months or so (assuming a three year term) the chances are you won't have to worry about your old property. The rent will, you hope, come close to making mortgage payments, and there will be someone in the house taking care of it.

At the end of about eighteen months, if the tenant/buyer feels they will be able to complete the purchase (perhaps a quarter of the time), you're set for another eighteen months and perhaps for good. On the other hand, if they don't and stop making payments, you can spend the money to have them evicted (since regardless of the option they are basically tenants, not owners). Then, if the market has turned around, you can resell, presumably for a good price. Or if it hasn't, you can try another lease option!

In short, as a desperation measure, it may work very well for you.

Combining Lease Option with Refinance

In the previous example, the seller used a lease option to get out of a property in order to move to a new city and buy another house. But how did he get his equity money out in order to buy another place?

The answer is the refinance. As long as you are the owner-occupant of a house, it's relatively easy to refinance for up to 80 percent of your house's current market value (not what it used to be worth). If you are thinking about doing a lease option, refinance first. (You'll have greater trouble trying to refinance after you move out and have a tenant move in.) This should get a substantial portion of your cash out (unless you bought recently and have only a little equity). Then do the lease option. You're away with some cash. It can be almost as good as selling.

As an alternative, if you don't want to refinance because of the increased mortgage payment charges, simply do the lease option and then rent in your new location. You can continue renting until the tenant/buyer of your old house exercises the option (if he does), and then when the old place sells (perhaps three years down the road), buy another place.

The lease option is a viable alternative for a seller who can't sell in a down market. In fact, it's a better alternative for the seller than for a prospective buyer. (If you don't know why, go back to the pluses and minuses. All the minuses remain for the buyer in a lease option with only one possible plus—locking in a price during a down market. However, since three-quarters of those who get a lease option fail to exercise it, even that plus is of dubious value to the buyer.)

Packaging

Packaging is a limited alternative for a few sellers. However, when it works, it can be a great way out of a serious problem, namely not being able to sell your property in a down market.

Understanding Packaging

A package is basically a group of properties put together and sold for their investment value. Investors, those with large sums of money to spend, often would like to own residential real estate. They would like, for example, to have ten good income producing properties in a given area. They especially want to buy these during a down market at low prices and then hang onto them until the market turns around.

However, such investors rarely have the time, patience, or enthusiasm to go out and find such properties, buy them, and then manage them. Rather, they'd prefer to have it all done for them.

That's where a packager comes in. The packager locates suitable properties and groups them together. He arranges financing for the purchase as well as management to see that the properties are rented out. Finally, he presents the package to potential buyers and, he hopes, one of them picks it up.

Packaging is neat, swift, and usually all cash to the seller. However, the big drawback is that often you can only get a minimal price for your house. However, if you have to sell and you want a quick way out, this might be it.

Finding a Packager

I'm sure many readers are saying to themselves, "What a good idea! Why didn't somebody else think of that? How do I get my hands on a packager?"

The answer, unfortunately, is that it's very hard to find a packager. Few people are doing it, and those who are tend to find you rather than the other way round. To understand why, consider the packager's perspective.

A typical packager is a real estate broker who has one or more wealthy clients. He tells these clients he has a way they can make big bucks out of today's depressed real estate market. (Brokers, are you listening?) With prices so depressed, he tells them residential property, houses, can be picked up for a song. The property can then be rented out for awhile, at least until the market turns around (as it surely will), and then resold for a huge profit. Of course, he will find the properties, arrange for the purchases, manage them, including finding tenants, and eventually sell them. All that's needed is for the wealthy client to put up the capital.

Since many wealthy people are also quite smart (that's how they got to be wealthy), they know the market will turn around eventually, and this is a good way to take advantage of it. So they agree.

Now, the agent has the sweetest deal ever to come down the pike. He arranges for the purchase of, say, ten houses to the wealthy client or a syndicate or corporation he forms. Along the way he collects ten commissions.

Then he rents the property for a period of years, collecting a management fee.

Finally, he sells all ten houses for a profit and again collects a commission, this time from the wealthy client. (As I said, brokers, are you listening?) It's easy to see why brokers like packaging.

Locating a Packager When You're a Seller

Okay, you understand the advantage to the wealthy client, the broker, and, of course, to you. But how do you connect up with a packager?

As I said, mostly they come looking for you. They are specifically looking for bargain basement property. They want houses at very low prices in areas with high rental rates. The idea is to buy a property that can be sustained by the rental income alone.

If you have a property that qualifies, but no packagers have come knocking at your door, you might let it be known to agents that you're willing to accept a package deal. Talk to as many agents as you can, even if your house is listed to only one, and spread the word. Many may simply not know what you're talking about. However, hopefully, someone in your area will talk to someone else, and one day a broker who's putting together a package will stop by.

Note: I don't think this is something for which you can advertise. However, if you know a wealthy person who would like to invest in real estate, you might be able to team up with a broker (it really does need a real estate license to pull it off), and put together a package, including your house, by yourself. Remember, necessity is the mother of invention, and when it's necessary to sell in a down market, you had better be plenty inventive.

Partnership

If you can't find a packager, the next best thing may be to put together a deal with just you and one investor—a partnership.

This alternative became popular a few years back under the name of "equity sharing." It was initiated by investors who wanted to take advantage of the skyrocketing real estate market in most areas of the country.

During the recent price decline, however, it has been relatively dormant. Now, however, with sellers needing to get out, it's undergoing a kind of rejuvenation. It's not without problems. But if you can deal with those, it might be a worthwhile solution for you.

Taking in a Partner

There are two ways a partnership arrangement could be helpful to you as a seller in a down market. We'll consider each separately. In the first case, you take in a partner.

In order to understand this application, it's important to keep track of your goals. What you really want in most cases is to get out of the property, with as much of your equity as possible, so you can go elsewhere, buy another house, or whatever. Taking in a partner could help you accomplish this.

The first step is to find a partner. This is a person who has three attributes:

Attributes of Your Partner

1. He or she wants to buy a house right away.
2. The partner makes a large enough amount of money to afford a substantial monthly payment.
3. He or she doesn't have any money for a down payment.

Where do you find such a person? One way is to advertise in the real estate section of your local paper. An ad which reads, "Investor Looking For Partner To Share Equity," will surely get you a lot of calls. (Remember, in this case, *you're* the investor since you own the property.) You might also find ads in which partners are looking for you, such as, "I'll Make Payments, You Handle Down—Shared Equity." You can also talk to real estate agents, mortgage brokers, and escrow officers. Sometimes they might know of a suitable partner for you.

Once you find someone who fits the bill, the next thing is to check them out. You want to be sure they do indeed have a big monthly income and aren't overburdened with other debt. You want them to be able to handle a mortgage on your house. A credit report is in order here.

Finally, when you're satisfied you've found the right party, you make them this offer: You will sell them a *half* interest in your house. They don't have to come up with any money; all they have to do is agree to live in the house for a set period of time, say for five years, and make all the mortgage, tax, and interest payments. At the end of the term, you'll both sell the house, and after your equity is returned to you, you'll split any profits.

If that sounds like a pretty good deal for the buyer, it is. They get into a house without it costing them a penny. All they have to do is make the monthly payments. At the end of a set period, the house is sold, and they get to split the profits. (They're going to have to make mortgage payments or pay rent somewhere, so why not let it be your place?) Even in today's down market, there are a great many people out there who want to buy, but can't because they simply don't have the down payment. Using this plan you tap into a vast resource of buyers previously unavailable to you.

It's also a pretty good deal for you. Here's how. You establish a fair market price for your house right now. With a down market it should be pretty low. Try to be realistic; it'll pay off later on down the road.

Now, transfer half the title to the property to your partner, and at the same time take out a new mortgage in the partner's name for as much as you can get, preferably 90 percent of the home's market value. (See chapter twelve for clues on financing.)

Once the new loan is in place, take the proceeds, pay off the existing loan, and put the balance in your pocket. Now, let your new half-owner partner move in and begin making payments.

You're off with most of your equity. If you got a 90 percent loan, you're leaving 10 percent of the sales price—your equity— behind. But you should recoup this when the property sells five or so years down the road. Remember, on sale your remaining equity comes out first, before any profits are divided.

If this sounds too good to be true, be aware that a great many people have successfully done equity sharing. However, a number of others have also had some problems.

Pitfalls of Taking in a Partner

There are a number of problems that may never arise, but conceivably could occur if you take in a partner. The biggest of these is that your partner might stop making the monthly payments he has agreed to make.

If He Stops Making Monthly Payments

Let's say that after the deal, property values decline even further. Your partner looks around and realizes that the agreed upon price for which he bought half your house is now $50,000 higher than comparable houses are going for. He's going to wonder just how good a deal he's got. And if he begins to think it's not that good a deal at all, he may simply say to heck with it, and stop making the payments.

What can you do about this? You have your equity to protect, assuming you still feel you have equity, given the above scenario. And you may have your credit to protect, if you signed as a co-mortgagor on the loan, which you probably did.

You can't evict your partner. Why not? Because he's not a tenant; he's an owner, and an owner can't be evicted. If your original partnership agreement (you should always have a written agreement document) provides for it, you can bring the matter to arbitration. Otherwise, it may have to go to court. Even if you win here, it could be months or even years before you get the house back and during that time, in order to protect your equity or credit, you'll have to keep making those monthly payments. If your partner doesn't move out, you can't even rent the property to recoup some of the costs!

About the only protection against this is to be sure your partner has a lot of assets so that if you win in court, as you probably would given the circumstances outlined (of course, nothing is guaranteed once matters get in the hands of lawyers and judges), you can collect damages. Of course, if your partner had assets to begin with, why would he have needed you?

Unusual Expenses

Another potential pitfall has to do with unusual expenses. What if a water pipe bursts and you have to repipe a portion of the house, something insurance won't cover. Or what if the house needs a new roof, a big expense. Does your partner pay it? Do you? Do you split it?

Since you're out of the house and off somewhere else, you certainly don't want to be responsible for paying for this. On the other hand, your partner, since he only owns half, isn't exactly going to be thrilled about paying for it, either.

There are several solutions here. If the market price for the house has fallen and your remaining equity has, for practical purposes, been wiped out, you might just sign over your half of the house to your partner in exchange for whatever your costs are. It won't cost you anything, and you'll be done with the property, but you will have lost your equity. (Be careful of recording a deed signing the property over to your partner. If you both signed for the mortgage, this could put you in default. You want to check with the mortgage lender to be sure they won't object. You could also be liable later on, if your partner defaults on the mortgage. But a letter explaining the circumstances along with a recorded deed to your partner may go a long way toward healing any credit illness you develop because of this problem.)

On the other hand, if you want to protect your equity, you can offer to take out a second mortgage on the property and share repayment with your partner. The money goes to pay to correct the problem. Or your partner can make the payments on the second, and when the property is sold, the second mortgage gets paid off before you get any equity out or any profits are split.

Or, you can simply pop for half the costs to correct the problem. Since cash is king in a down market, I would suggest this last is the least desirable solution for you.

Improper Documents

Next, you need a rock solid contract that spells out all the terms and conditions of your partnership, and that provides ways for dealing with problems such as those described above. For this you need a first-rate real estate attorney. A word of warning here: There are several books out on the market that discuss equity sharing and contain prepared contract forms. While these forms may be the basis for a contract, I wouldn't rely on them exclusively. Take them to your attorney so he or she can adapt them to your special needs. Anyone who copies a form out of a book and then uses it to equity share is just asking for trouble.

Tax Consequences

Finally, there's the matter of tax consequences. When you sell half your house, can you roll over the gain using the deferral of principal residence rule discussed elsewhere in the book? Probably, but you may only be able to defer half the gain. This is a matter for your tax attorney.

Also, what about the deduction taken on income taxes for mortgage interest and taxes? Who gets it? You or your partner?

Normally, the person who actually pays gets the deduction. In this case it would be your partner. But a clever real estate attorney or CPA might be able to structure the deal so that you can get part or even all of these deductions. This benefit alone might be worth more, over time, than your remaining equity in the property!

This, then, is how to get out by taking in a partner. However, when we started I mentioned there were two ways a partnership might be helpful to you. The first, as we've seen, is to take in a partner. The second is to sell outright to a partnership.

Sell to a Partnership

In a variation of the above scenario, instead of taking in a partner, you find two partners. On the one hand you find someone with cash who wants to invest, such as in our earlier technique of packaging. Then, you find someone, like the partner above, who can make the monthly payments, who wants to buy, but who has no cash. Put them together with your house as the wedding ring, and you're out.

As with most things in life, however, this is harder than it seems. It is difficult enough to find a wealthy individual who wants to work with a packager. But it can be equally difficult to find an individual who wants to put up cash to equity share in a down market.

The reasons should be obvious. The market could drop, thus wiping out the investor's equity. The partner might not make payments, putting the investor at more risk. There might be unexpected costs, or the documents could be faulty.

This is not to say it's impossible to find an investor who might join someone who can make payments to buy your property. But I wouldn't start spending my equity until the escrow closed.

One other thing. While you put all this together, keep in mind that since you're not a partner, the other two don't really need you. There's nothing to prevent them from going off and buying some other house! It's just one more thing to worry about.

Time-Sharing

Time-sharing is a very specific and limited way out, and it only applies if your property has some sort of special use value. By special use I mean it is recreational property or in the downtown area of a city people might want to visit . . . or some similar situation.

The idea here is that you take in a whole bunch of partners. You sell them each a portion of the property, and then allow them to use it a portion of the time. An example should help to clarify it.

Let's suppose you have a house in a wildlife area near a river where there's good fishing. You were living in the area because it's where your job was located. But you've had a job change and must move elsewhere. Only in today's down market, you can't sell.

So you set up a time-share arrangement. You find five or ten or more people who are interested in fishing and owning part of a recreational property. You get together with them and split up the year. If it's six people, for example, they can each have it for two months, not necessarily all in one stretch. A new deed is drawn naming all the owners, usually as tenants in common (see your attorney for information on how to set up the title). There's a special time-sharing contract drafted and signed by all the owners. And usually there is new financing put on the property so you can get all of your cash out. (You get your equity out in part from the new financing and the remainder from the down payments the time-sharers put up.)

Let's say you have a house you are trying to sell for $150,000 in a recreational area. You decide to time-share it. You sell a total of five shares for $30,000 apiece. Each person puts up $5,000 in cash and agrees to make payments on the remaining balance of $25,000. In exchange they get to use the property two months a year. (This is actually how time-sharing was first conceived in France—a small group of individuals sharing a property none of them could otherwise afford.)

Consider the deal. Five other people put up $30,000 for a total of $150,000, your selling price. They put enough cash in to equal a down payment and agree to make payments on a new loan you secure. You, in effect, sell your house for cash—get all your cash out from either the down payment or the new loan. But, as an additional partner, you retain the right to use it for two months a year . . . without any cost or monthly payments to you! (After all, there should be some profit to you for putting together this fairly complex deal.)

Of course, you could share equally in costs, cash, and payments with your partners if you chose to. In any event, no matter how you do it, rest assured that others are doing it as well. The keys are a piece of property others want to visit for recreational purposes, or want to visit in a city part time on business (such as a downtown condo), and a good time-sharing agreement that locks everyone in and likewise offers them each solid protection. (Be sure you see a competent real estate attorney for this.)

As I noted at the beginning, a time-share sale isn't for every property. But if you have one that does have time-share potential, why not go that way? If it works, you can not only sell your house in a down market, but retain the right to use it part time as well!

9

When to Bail Out

When most people buy a home, it's with the anticipation of staying in it a long time. Certainly some of us do buy only for the short term, particularly if we know our job will force us to move in a few years or if we're speculating on price. But for the vast majority of home buyers, the commitment of a large down payment and a mortgage stretching out for what seems like the rest of our lives is a commitment to stay put.

This is expressed in many ways, but is clearly seen when we buy, move in, and "fix up the house." This isn't to imply the house we bought was necessarily run down. Rather, it's a matter of taking psychological ownership. We paint colors we like. We add wallpaper, change cabinets, add new flooring, improve a room, or redecorate a bath or kitchen.

The amount of money most homeowners spend "fixing up" a house so it becomes just the way they like it usually far exceeds what would be justified solely on the basis of investment. But most of us don't care if we'll ever get our money out. We want the house to feel like our home, our security, our own special place.

In a Down Market

All of the above sits well with most of us as long as our home goes up in value, or at least holds its price. But how do we feel when our home's value begins to decline? Lower prices make us begin to reevaluate our commitment to our house.

This is certainly the case when housing prices decline to the point where our home is worth less than the cost of selling it. In many areas of the country, particularly in the Northeast and Southwest, people who bought homes only two or three years ago, when prices were high, are now finding the values of those homes have dipped sharply lower. Today, they discover, if they were to sell that home, they would net out virtually nothing after paying off the mortgage and the costs of the sale.

It's a terrible feeling to know the house you're living in, on which you may have made a $20,000 to $50,000 down payment, and into which you've poured huge amounts of money in monthly payments, not to mention the money you spent fixing it up, isn't worth anything.

When Your House Becomes Worthless

The sad truth is that in many places in this country, home owners are faced with exactly this dilemma. The house they bought is no longer worth anything to them. Falling prices have erased their equity.

For many people this poses a real dilemma. On the one hand they want to fix up their home, to take psychological ownership. On the other, they realize they are pouring money down a bottomless pit. It's one thing to fantasize that the money you spend fixing up your home may not be completely justified, but the price is going up, and someday you'll get it out, anyhow. It's quite another to see prices going down and realize you may never get out the money you are spending today.

At some point any reasonable person has to ask these questions:

Should I keep fixing this place up?
Should I keep this place?
Should I bail out?

Making the Decision to Bail Out

Back in 1988 when the market was probably at its low point in Texas, a great many homeowners were facing this exact problem. Grace was one of them.

She bought her three bedroom, two bath house five years earlier, when prices were still high. She paid close to $90,000 for it and felt it was both a good investment and a good place to live. She immediately began fixing up the place, painting and papering to fit her tastes. She put in a new lawn, new fencing, and a spa in the back yard. In short, she transformed the house into a home.

Then came the fallout in Texas real estate. Prices began to drop. Houses nearby Grace's were soon selling for $85,000, then $80,000.

Grace had put $20,000 down and had a $70,000 mortgage. She was concerned about falling prices, but not alarmed. She figured (correctly over the long haul) that what went down would eventually come back up.

But prices continued to slip. Soon houses nearby were selling for $75,000, and then, in one amazing fall, they were down to $55,000. If she wanted to, Grace could buy the house right next door to hers, a spitting image of her own home, for $15,000 less than she owed on her own mortgage!

Grace was appalled. Where was her $20,000 down, not to mention the money she had spent fixing up the place? More importantly, how much sense did it make to keep on making those mortgage payments? She was currently paying $650 in principle and interest. If she bought the house next door, her monthly mortgage payments would drop to just over $400! She could save $250 every month just by moving next door.

Should Grace move out?

Or should she stay and keep hoping for the best?

We'll find out shortly what Grace actually did. Along the way, however, I hope you'll be able to pick up some insights about what you could do in your specific situation. In a falling market, even if you aren't forced to sell, you too may be wondering whether you should bail out simply because prices have fallen too low.

Here are some answers that helped Grace, and should help you, to make this decision.

Timing

By the time most of us reach the age of thirteen, we realize that life is a crapshoot. "You pays your money and you takes your chances" are probably among the truest words ever spoken, and they certainly apply to real estate in a down market.

When you see the prices falling around you, should you sell now, even at a loss (that is, less than you could have got yesterday or last year), or should you hold, waiting until times get better?

If you sell, you won't get as much money as you think your home is worth. But, if you hold, you could find the prices continue to fall until, at some point, as in the case of Grace, your entire equity is wiped out. When do you decide it's the right time to bail out?

I have seen some real estate writers give formulas here:

"When you've lost half your equity and prices are still falling, get out or you'll lose it all!"

Or, "As soon as prices start down, bail out!"

Or, "Hang on indefinitely, if you can. Eventually the market will have to get better."

All of this advice contains grains of truth. The problem, however, is that most of it fails to take into consideration the emotional attachment many of us feel toward our homes. It's not like talking about a stock, bond, commodity, or other investment. It's easy to decide to bail out on them, because we're not emotionally committed to them.

But our home is something different. While it might make good economic sense to get out early before the bottom drops out of the market, it might make bad emotional sense.

Therefore, with regard to timing a bail out in a down market, I suggest the following:

1. As soon as possible, after the market turns sour, begin looking at other homes.

The reasoning here has more to do with emotion than with getting a fix on the real estate market. When you look at other homes, you cannot help but compare them with your own. Some comparisons will be favorable, but others will not. When you see things you like in other homes, you will begin to notice things (probably never before considered) you don't really like in your current home. Along the way, you'll begin to put emotional distance between you and your house. You'll begin to prepare yourself to leave, if it becomes necessary.

2. Read everything you can on your local real estate market.

You don't have to be a real estate broker or an economist to know how well or how badly things are going. Will Rogers said, "Everything I know I learned by reading the newspapers." You can learn everything you need to know about the real estate market by reading your local papers. It will print reports of housing starts and home sales. It will have comments from leading economists and brokers. In short, it will tell you how the market's doing right now, and what the prospects are for the future. If all the signs point downward toward doom and gloom, you should realize that you may have to take some sort of action before long.

3. Keep track of your equity.

Your equity is the amount of your money in your home. It is found simply by taking the price for which you could sell your home and subtracting your mortgage and your costs of sale. (Note: your equity may be considerably different from your taxable "gain.") Here's how to figure your equity:

Calculating Your Home Equity

Anticipated sales price		$ 100,000
Less		
Mortgage	$ 50,000	
Commission	6,000	
Other sales costs	<u>3,000</u>	
	59,000	<u>-59,000</u>
Your equity		41,000

Each time the price of your house goes down, as measured by the decline of sales prices of comparable houses, your anticipated sales price should also go down, and so will your equity.

4. Watch for important milestones.

There are certain events that should suggest now may be the time to bail out in your mind. Here is a list of those you should watch out for:

Milestones to Watch Out For

- When prices first begin to drop (instead of appreciating or stabilizing).
- When prices fall below what you originally paid for your home.
- When half your *original* equity is wiped out.
- When all your *original* equity is wiped out.
- When you owe more than the amount for which you can sell your home.

In a declining market, you could conceivably go through all of the stages noted above. At each stage, you have to ask yourself, should I sell now? Or should I hang on? For the remainder of this chapter, we'll consider the consequences of doing either for each stage.

Bailing Out When Prices First Begin to Drop

This is the hardest time of all to sell in a down market (although no time is easy). You've seen prices go up, then stabilize, and now the local newspaper (and perhaps agents with whom you talk) tell you prices are getting "soft." The market is "sluggish." Homes have been for sale a long time and just aren't moving.

The tendency here is to want to wait and hold. You may be saying to yourself, "I should have sold last month (or six months ago, or last year). I missed the top of the market. Well, I'll just have to wait until things get better."

The problem, of course, as we've seen, is that they may get a lot worse before they get any better. It may turn out that if you sell right now, even at a small loss, you'll still be doing a lot better than if you hang on until later, when to sell you could take a big loss. How do you make the decision?

My suggestion is that if you can afford not to sell, try and stick it out. You presumably did not buy your home strictly as an investment. Therefore, you should not be sensitive to minor fluctuations in price, up or down.

Yes, it could be the beginning of a long price drop, and selling at once could be the smart thing to do. But if you sell, what are you going to do then? Rent? Buy another home (which puts you right back where you were)?

If it were me (and it has been), I'd choose to stay put, for the time being.

Bailing Out When Prices Fall Below What You Originally Paid for Your Home

A lot depends on when you bought. This is usually a big problem, primarily for people who bought fairly recently, within the previous three to five years.

In most markets there was a big price hike just before things turned around. On the West Coast, for example, during 1988 and 1989, prices in some areas increased by as much as fifty percent.

If you were one of those unfortunate enough to buy during this peaking period, you know exactly what it feels like to watch prices drop below what you paid. You bought at the top, and when the price roller coaster heads for a trough, you're the first to notice the pinch.

On the other hand, *if you bought years ago,* it's a different story. Here, I suggest you go back to the time just before the most recent price spike. Let's say you bought years ago for $40,000. But just two years ago, your home could have been sold for $80,000. Then last year the price spiked to $100,000. Should you be concerned when prices fall below $100,000? Or when they fall below $80,000? Or below $40,000?

My suggestion is to worry when they fall below $80,000. The spike to $100,000 was just a temporary move and can be dismissed. Chances are that unless you sold during the one month at the peak of the market, you probably couldn't have got $100,000 anyhow. The $40,000 price you originally paid is so old as to be irrelevant, for our purposes here.

In short, as soon as prices drop below the most recent realistic value of your property (or what you paid for it if you bought only a short time ago), it's time to consider bailing out. As soon as your equity begins to be worn away as described above, you must ask yourself, "Is it time to move on? If I stay here, will I lose more money?"

My suggestion is that as soon as you see your equity drop (determined by either what you paid or your most recent realistic appreciated value), you panic. Remember, in the 1990s cash is king. Because of government and private borrowing, everyone is going to be short of cash. Those who have it, on the other hand, can write their own ticket. Are you now willing to see that most precious commodity, cash (in the form of equity), eroded? Keep in mind that if you lose your equity, you may lose your ability to buy another home now or for a long time to come.

If it were me, as soon as prices had dropped to the point where my equity was threatened, I would seriously consider selling. If the market is that bad, then chances are I could do quite well just by getting my equity out and sticking it in a bank where it could gain interest. I could rent for a time, and then, when the market was near the bottom, buy another home.

True, there's the risk that the market might turn right around as soon as I sold, and I would have lost money by selling. But, just as likely it might fall even farther, and if I have my equity out, I'll then be in a position to buy a house for next to nothing.

Bailing Out When Half Your *Original* Equity Is Wiped Out

If you wait until half your original equity ("original" means the amount you stuck into the property) is wiped out, in my opinion, you waited too long.

At this point, assuming the market is still going down, there should be little question. The right *economic* move is probably to bail out immediately. (Of course, as noted earlier, it may not be possible for you to do this from a psychological perspective.)

If you stick it out much longer, you may see the loss of your entire equity. If you originally put in $30,000, and now your interest in the property is down to $15,000, unless you sell, it well may soon be down to zero. On the theory that, in this market, cash is better than anything else, it's better to have $15,000 in cash than nothing.

I would sell.

Bailing Out When All Your *Original* Equity Is Wiped Out

Now you know you waited too long. If you originally put $30,000 in the property and were to try to sell today, you would get zero out.

You now have to ask yourself, what's the advantage of selling? If you sell now you'll get nothing. Isn't it better, therefore, to stay put?

The answer is yes . . . and no.

If you feel the most you can lose is all you put in, and you've already lost that, then perhaps staying in the house and continuing to make payments does make sense. You can't lose anymore, you hope. After all, it will certainly cost something to move, even if you move to a rental.

On the other hand, if you feel there is yet more to lose, then perhaps selling, even at a loss, does make sense. You have to consider the alternatives. Prices could stay right where they are (unlikely), or they could move up—or further down.

If they move down, and you're forced to move later on, you could end up not being able to sell at all. You could conceivably lose the house to foreclosure. A good piece of advice an old broker once told me is, "Never underestimate market conditions. Things can always get better . . . or worse!"

Let's consider the pros and cons:

Pro: With your equity gone, you have nothing to lose by selling. As it is, you're simply paying rent to live in your home. (Chances are, in fact, you could rent your home, or one almost identical to it, for less than you're currently paying in mortgage payments!) Selling gives you a fresh start, perhaps in a different area where things aren't so bad.

Con: If you sell, you lose everything you put into the house. You lose your equity, the amount of your mortgage payment that went into principle, any improvements you made, your costs of purchase, and so forth. If you don't sell, on the other hand, you can at least hope there will be a turnaround somewhere down the road and prices will come back.

I can't suggest what you should do here. It's a call you have to make based on your gut feelings.

Bailing Out When You're Upside Down

"Upside down" means you owe more than the amount for which you can sell your home. This, of course, is the toughest situation of all. Here, you owe more than your house is worth, the situation Grace found herself in.

It's an excruciating position to be in. On the one hand, you can simply sit tight and hope for the best. Chances are that someday things will turn around and prices will go back up.

On the other hand, every day you will drive and walk by houses that are essentially the same as yours, only that cost less. People who do buy them and move in may prove to be from lower economic levels and may not share your interests. You may find, in short, that because prices have dropped, your neighborhood and the people in it have changed. You may find you'd just rather not be living there any more.

A large part of your decision, of course, will be based on what you can do. If, for example, you have a mortgage of $80,000 and your home is only worth $60,000, how do you bail out?

Keep in mind that if you choose to sell, the only way you can give clear title to a buyer is to pay off the mortgage. To do that, you'll have to come up with $20,000, plus closing costs and commission, if any! That's not an alternative most people will consider realistic by any stretch of the imagination. On the other hand, if you just walk away from the house, your credit could be ruined as the lender puts the house into foreclosure, and in some cases you could be liable for any loss the lender sustains. (We'll cover this in detail in the next chapter.)

I can only tell you what I would personally do, and that is to bail out, quickly. (Again, see the next chapter for suggestions on how to lessen the blow.)

Moving Away

If the truth be known, almost all of us are short term owners. Back in the 1970s the average length of home ownership nationwide was around eight years. By the 1980s that had dropped to only seven years. In some highly mobile areas, such as California, the rate of house hopping has been closer to five years.

What this means is that regardless of how emotionally attached to our house or how much we might have to lose when we sell, no matter what, the chances are we really won't stay there forever. Even if times were good, our economic situation might change, or our employment might require a move, or our family may grow up and away, leaving us with a house that's just too big. In short, no matter what the market, chances are that sooner or later, almost all of us will want to sell the house we're in and move elsewhere.

This is not to say that when times get rough you should automatically move. It is to say, however, that you shouldn't feel wedded to your home. Sometimes, as we've seen, in a down market, bailing out and moving is, indeed, the right thing to do.

Which brings us back to the story of Grace. Did she bail out? The answer is, no! She is still living in that house, still hoping the market will turn around and she will recoup her losses.

Did she make the right move? She thinks she did and, if she lives long enough, I'm sure the market will prove her right.

10

How to Avoid Foreclosure

When Harry and Jenny bought their southern California home in 1988, they anticipated a relaxed life style, lots of backyard barbecues, and ever increasing equity. Life, however, had planned a few twists.

Within three months after their purchase, the Orange County residential market (previously one of the strongest in the nation) collapsed. Housing prices stalled, then began to nose downward.

What was worse, in order to make the purchase on the high priced California home, they both had to work. Their purchase price had been close to $300,000, and their monthly payments were roughly $2,500 with taxes and insurance. But in 1990, they both were laid off. Harry had worked for Hughes Aircraft in El Segundo, but he was caught in a round of cut-backs. Jenny worked for a title insurance company near their home, but with reduced sales, her job was eliminated in a cost cutting effort.

For the first few months they were optimistic, making their payments out of savings and severance pay. Harry was an engineer and felt he would have little trouble getting a new job. But he hadn't reckoned on the cut-backs in all defense-related industries. There simply were no new jobs available to him. Jenny quickly got a secretarial job to help make ends meet, but her salary was far less than it had been at the title insurance company.

Soon the new realities came home to them both. There was no way they could continue to make $2,500 a month payments. Their best bet, in fact, was to sell the house and move to another area . . . perhaps Seattle or even the South, where many manufacturers and defense contractors were relocating.

So they put their house up for sale. Only by now the market had completely collapsed. They had bought at the very peak of the market. They were told that in order to sell now, at or near the bottom, they would have to offer their home for around $230,000, fully $70,000 less than they had paid only two years earlier.

Besides the big drop in market prices, the problem was that they had only put down twenty percent, the standard down payment. It had amounted to $60,000. They still owed $240,000, fully $10,000 less than the amount they had been told they could sell the place for! (And that didn't take into account commission and closing costs.) In short, to sell, it would cost them roughly $20,000 out of their pocket.

Harry was mad about the whole thing. "We've been taken," he said. "The original agent talked us into paying more than we should have. Our old companies flaked out on us by letting us go after making long-term employment commitments to us. And now brokers want to take advantage of us by forcing us to sell at a loss. To heck with them. Let's just walk out of here and start over someplace else!"

Harry's attitude was certainly understandable. However, Jenny wasn't so sure it was the best thing to do. She rightly reasoned that what happened to them really wasn't anyone's fault. Economic conditions had simply changed, and they had caught the brunt of that change.

Further, how well they could start someplace else might be directly affected by the way they got out of their present situation. If they simply walked away, the mortgage company would have little choice but to foreclose and take the property back. If it did that, the foreclosure would surely follow them and make it more difficult for them to get future credit, as well as to qualify for a mortgage on a new home. Wasn't there a better alternative, she wondered?

Jenny's concern was well placed. Allowing a foreclosure to occur on their property could ruin the couple's credit and ability to purchase another home for years to come.

In this chapter we are going to look into the consequences of foreclosure and how to avoid them. Hopefully, your situation won't be quite as severe as that of Jenny and Harry. However, anytime foreclosure is threatened, you should know you are in big trouble.

What Happens If You Lose a House to Foreclosure

We'll go into the actual steps involved in foreclosure shortly. However, first let's consider what happens when foreclosure actually takes place.

The final step in foreclosure, usually, is when your property is sold "on the courthouse steps" to the highest bidder. Typically the highest bidder is the mortgage company since it, after all, has the entire mortgage in the property.

In the old days, that is, more than twenty years ago, about the only people who knew you had gone through foreclosure were you and the mortgage company. Yes, anyone checking through the county records could come up with the foreclosure information, but there were few who actually checked. Specifically, the three major national credit reporting agencies did not check the county records. (They still rarely do.)

Consequently, some people who had gone through foreclosure, as long as their other credit remained sound, could go out and almost immediately apply for and obtain a mortgage on another property. When they came to the question on the new mortgage application which asked, "Have you ever lost a property through foreclosure?" they would lie and answer, "No," and chances are no one would be the wiser! (This is not to advocate lying on the application. Such lying would constitute fraud and could have severe criminal and civil penalties.)

That, however, was before computerization. Now, all institutional mortgage lenders (who make up about 97 percent of the first mortgages) are computerized. As soon as you are several months behind in your mortgage payments, they tend to report this information to the credit rating bureaus. If they foreclose on your home, this information is also reported, and, hence, any new lender who asks for a credit report will get it.

Since it is standard practice to refuse a new mortgage to any applicant who has had a foreclosure in the previous seven to ten years, your chances of getting a new mortgage and being able to buy a new house are severely reduced (but not eliminated, as we'll see shortly) once foreclosure has occurred.

In addition, your credit in general will suffer. This could take the form of having credit denied as well as having existing lines of credit reduced or eliminated.

In short, a foreclosure, though not as severe as a bankruptcy, will have a serious effect on your credit.

The way to avoid the problems caused by having a foreclosure on your record is to avoid the foreclosure in the first place. That is what we will look into for the remainder of this chapter.

The Foreclosure Timetable

Before actually going forward in understanding how to avoid a foreclosure, it's important that you understand the timetable. Foreclosure does not happen overnight. It takes time for the lender to foreclose, and there are specific steps the lender must take. At each step you have a specific recourse, if you choose and are able to use it.

The timetable for foreclosure depends on the state you are in. Foreclosure is governed by state, not federal law. While the state laws vary, almost all fit within two categories: trust deeds (the most widely used mortgage instrument) and mortgages (the older mortgage instrument). Any real estate agent can tell you which instrument is used in your state. Indeed, you can tell simply by looking at the documents you received when you purchased your home. (Note: the terms "mortgage" and "trust deed" are used synonymously in this book, except in this section.)

Trust Deed Foreclosure

The general steps in foreclosing on a trust deed are the notification, the redemption period, the advertising period, and the sale. The time frame varies, as noted, from state to state. For our example, we'll pick California, which is the model for most other states' trust deed instruments.

A trust deed has three parties. There's you, the borrower or "trustor." There's the lender, technically called the "beneficiary." And then there's an independent third party, usually a title insurance company, called the "trustee."

When you borrow you actually sign title of your property over to the trustee. The trustee has the power to sell your property anytime you default or don't pay the mortgage. Of course, a strict procedure has to be followed. But once the beneficiary (lender) notifies the trustee that you're in default, the foreclosure clock starts running, and when it runs down, the trustee sells your home to the highest bidder.

Note that in a trust deed, there is no need of judicial foreclosure. That means the lender does *not* have to go to court to foreclose. This saves time for the lender and accounts for the popularity of this instrument.

Note: In a trust deed judicial foreclosure is allowed if the lender so chooses. A lender might want to do this since judicial foreclosure allows for a deficiency judgement. If your house cannot be sold for the amount of the loan, a deficiency judgement means you could be liable for the difference! We'll have more to say about this, later.

Trust Deed Countdown

Here are the steps involved in foreclosure if you have a trust deed:

Default

Default means that you aren't making your trust deed payments. Typically the payment will be due on the first of the month. If you don't pay by the fifteenth or later, a penalty will be added, usually about five percent of the monthly payment. At the end of thirty days, you are in default. (Technically you are in default on the second day of the month that you don't pay, since home loan payments are made after the interest is due. This is opposed to renting, where you pay a month in advance.)

Usually at this stage nothing much will happen. The lender may send you a notice reminding you your payment is past due and politely ask you to look into your records to see if you forgot to make it. This is typically the case if you've been making your payments regularly.

During the second month after you stop making payments, you can expect to get a call from the lender asking for an explanation. If you reply courteously to this call and report that you have some short-term financial problems, you may be let off with a rebuke. The lender may threaten to report your late payments and ruin your credit. But, if you promise to pay soon, chances are nothing much will happen.

In general, savings and loans and banks, who represent 90 percent of all first trust deed lenders, don't have to report a loan on their books as non-performing until interest has not been paid for 90 days. Thus, if you hold out the hope to them that you will pay soon, chances are for three months at least they'll do nothing except threaten.

How long a lender will wait depends on the lender. When regulators were less strict in times past, sometimes you could get away with six or nine months before the next step in foreclosure was taken. More recently with tougher regulations, about three months is the most you probably can delay the process.

A Private Lender or the RTC

An exception here is if the lender is a private individual or the Resolution Trust Corporation (RTC). A private individual isn't worried about reporting non-performing loans. He or she only wants to get paid and may move forward with the next step of foreclosure immediately.

The RTC, which has taken over many failed S&Ls, likewise is only concerned about getting paid, and may not wait at all before moving forward with the next step.

Notice of Default

The next step comes when the lender files a "notice of default." This is a legally required step that puts you on official notice that you're not making your payments. The notice is recorded and published in a legal newspaper.

You now have a set period of time during which you can make your loan good. In California the time period is three months. In other states the time will vary—check with a local attorney or real estate agent. (Some states do not have this waiting period.)

This time period is called your redemption time. The reason is that you can redeem the loan, without the approval of the lender, simply by making up all back payments, penalties, and costs. (The penalties are the late charges that occur each month, and the costs are the attorney fees the lender has incurred in filing the notice of default—usually fairly small.)

During this three month period you may not even hear from the lender. But don't let the lack of attention lull you into a false sense of security. The clock is ticking. You are getting ever closer to losing your property.

What to Do during the Redemption Period

What should you do during this period? If possible, you should be seeking out ways of either selling the house to someone else, who will pay off the loan, or trying to get the funds to remedy the default, perhaps by securing new financing.

One other thing you should do is to hire a good real estate attorney. He should carefully examine the notice of default you received. He will check it over for accuracy. The property's legal address must be correct, as must your name and the terms of the loan. If the lender made a mistake in issuing the notice of default, your attorney can go to court and have it quashed. This would mean the lender would have to file again, giving you more time. (Yes, lenders do make mistakes with surprising frequency. This is even more the case with the larger workload they face today with ever increasing numbers of foreclosures. What they count on is that most borrowers never bother to check the documents that are filed!)

Publishing Notice of Sale

Once the redemption period has run out (three months in California), you can no longer redeem your loan. You could walk in with all the back payments, penalties, and costs, and the lender could simply refuse to accept it. In short, you've lost the mortgage. The only question remaining is, will you lose the property?

In order to sell your house, the trustee must now give formal notice of the sale. This is done by advertising the sale in a legal newspaper. In California, the sale must be advertised for a minimum of three weeks. The advertisement must notify the public of the time and place of the sale.

During this time frame your recourses are limited. You can completely pay off the loan, including penalties and costs. This doesn't mean just making up back payments. It means paying off the *entire* amount you borrowed.

Sometimes this is feasible, if during the previous redemption period you somehow managed to talk a different lender into giving you a new loan. A new lender might do this if you could demonstrate otherwise sound credit and a new job, as well as a good reason for your property being in default.

Again, your attorney could challenge the publication notice, but this at best would be only a short-term delaying tactic.

Or, if you did come up with the money to make up back mortgage payments, you could ask the lender to reinstate the loan.

This last could work better than most people assume. The reason is that the lender doesn't want your property back. It certainly doesn't want it back if the value has dropped below the loan amount. In this event, the lender may even be willing to reinstate the loan if you only make interest payments and may forego penalties and costs! Remember, however, this is done only at the discretion of the lender; you have no right to demand reinstatement.

Foreclosure Sale

Then your property is sold "on the courthouse steps" to the highest bidder.

You can bid. Of course, you have to bid more than the lender, who will bid the amount of the loan plus lost interest, costs, and penalties.

However, assuming you do not bid, you have lost your house irredeemably. In a property sold in this fashion you have no "equity of redemption": you can never come back and redeem the house by paying back interest or costs. The house is now the property of the lender and no longer yours.

If you are still in possession, the lender can have you immediately evicted through an unlawful detainer action, and you could be liable for the costs of this procedure.

The purpose of going through the details of this procedure, however, is not to scare you, but to make you aware of the timetable involved. If you don't know the timetable, then you can't take timely steps. Later in this chapter, we'll consider alternatives that can stop foreclosure. First, however, let's consider the other major loan instrument, the mortgage, and see how its timetable works.

Mortgage Countdown

The general procedure for foreclosing on a mortgage is the judicial process. The mortgage is accelerated by the lender, there is a complaint filed with the court, a hearing, a judgement, and finally a redemption period. The time frame varies from state to state and between judicial districts.

Unlike a trust deed, a mortgage has only two parties. There's you, the mortgagor, and there's the lender, the mortgagee.

Note that unlike with a trust deed, there is the strong possibility of a "deficiency judgement": if your house cannot be sold for the amount of the loan, you could be liable for the difference!

Here are the steps if you are faced with foreclosure of a mortgage:

Acceleration

The lender accelerates the mortgage. As soon as you stop making payments, the mortgagee has the right to call in the entire mortgage. Usually this takes the form of a letter to you stating that because you have failed to make your payments, the entire mortgage is now due and payable.

This does not mean, however, that you've lost your property yet or anything even close to it. You can contact the lender and explain your difficulties. As I've noted, lenders are not eager to take back properties during this period.

The lender may be willing to negotiate with you. You may be able to extend the term of the mortgage, get reduced payments for a period, get payments waived for a short period, refinance the mortgage, or anything else. In short, depending on your negotiating abilities and the lender's desire to avoid foreclosure, the sky's the limit. You should make every effort to contact the lender and to see if something can't be worked out.

Complaint Filed

Once you are more than 90 days in arrears (see the earlier section on bank reporting of non-paying loans), or once the lender has given up hope of your being able to make your mortgage right, it may file a complaint with the court. You will receive a summons.

You must answer the summons, and you should seek the counsel of a real estate attorney. Simply ignoring the summons won't make it go away.

If you acknowledge that the mortgage is indeed right, you are behind in payments, penalties and costs, the lender can file for a summary judgement. This is heard before a judge and can result in your quickly losing your house.

You are, however, entitled to your day in court. You can protest the action on whatever grounds your attorney advises, and then a trial date will be set.

The trial date depends on the court's docket, but foreclosures often take precedence over other civil cases, and you may find it set within a month or so. On the other hand, in a crowded court it may take six months or longer. As noted, you will need the services of an attorney here.

At the trial the mortgagee will present evidence to sustain its claim that you are in default on your mortgage. You, through your attorney, may present evidence that the mortgagee would not accept payment, that the documents were in error, that there were extenuating circumstances, or whatever.

Unless there were true errors made, however, the outcome is usually a foregone conclusion. A foreclosure judgement will be given to the mortgagee.

Judgement Sale

The judgement can now be recorded, and the lender can sell your home, after advertising, "on the courthouse steps." If you protest, the court may also appoint a referee to examine the situation further.

At the appointed day, the house is sold. You can bid. Of course, you have to bid more than the lender, who will bid the amount of the loan plus lost interest, costs, and penalties.

However, assuming you do not bid, you have lost your house, but not irredeemably. In a property sold in this fashion you usually have an equity of redemption: you can come back and redeem the house by paying off the mortgage amount, back interest, and costs.

The time period for your redemption varies by state, but can be as long as a year or more. During this time, the lender normally has possession of your property and may, indeed, sell it to someone else, subject to your equity of redemption.

Notice the difference between foreclosure in a trust deed and in a mortgage. In a trust deed the redemption period occurs *before* the foreclosure sale. In a mortgage, it occurs *afterward*.

If you are still in possession, the lender can have you immediately evicted through an unlawful detainer action, and, again, you could be liable for the costs of this procedure.

Deficiency Judgements

If your house cannot be sold for the amount you owe, the lender, in some cases, may secure a deficiency judgement against you for its loss. For example, say you owe $85,000 including costs and back interest. But the property can only be sold for $70,000. The lender may be able to secure a judgement against you for the $15,000 difference. You could be required to pay this out of your other personal or real property. For example, the money could be taken out of a bank account or your car could be sold.

A deficiency judgement, however, can only be obtained when your property was lost through judicial foreclosure. In other words, if you had a trust deed and the property was sold by a trust deed sale (as most are), no deficiency judgement is possible.

Keep in mind, however, that in a down market with prices falling, some lenders elect (as is usually their right) to foreclose a trust deed through court. In that case a deficiency judgement is possible.

Purchase Money Laws

Many states have enacted purchase money laws. These are intended to prevent injustices where someone buys a house and then, because he couldn't afford it, loses it through foreclosure. If your state has a purchase money law, it means that no deficiency judgement can be secured against you even if the lender goes through judicial foreclosure provided the mortgage was *part of the purchase price*. Check with a local real estate attorney or agent to see whether your state has a purchase money law on the books.

Things to Do to Avoid Foreclosure

These then are the consequences of foreclosure and how the foreclosure procedure works. All of this information is vital to you if you are being foreclosed upon. However, what is of even more importance is defeating the foreclosure. How do you do that? We'll find out in the rest of the chapter.

Challenge the Foreclosure

As noted in several places, you can challenge the foreclosure, regardless of the procedure used, at each step of the way. Lenders are notorious for making errors in filing documents. If you challenge each document each step of the way, it can, if nothing else, delay the proceedings for many months.

If you decide on this option, be sure you have your attorney also examine and challenge the original loan documents. In some cases these are improperly drawn. If they were, they may be unenforceable! Further, in some rare cases not only might they be unenforceable, but if you were economically damaged by the way they were drawn, the lender can be responsible for damages! It's certainly worth the time to make the examination.

Contact the Lender

This is equally important. If the lender writes you letters and phones you, and you never return the call or messages, the lender can only assume you don't want to pay. It has little recourse but to foreclose.

On the other hand, if you contact the lender and explain your situation, the lender may actually be able to help! Remember, the last thing the lender wants in a down market is to take back your house.

If, as in our original example of Harry and Jenny, the lender learns you've lost your job, but you anticipate finding a new job in a relatively short period of time, it may be willing to wait. On the other hand, if you find a job, but it's for less than you were previously making, the lender may be willing to actually advance you some money to consolidate other bills so your total monthly payment is less.

Remember, if the lender can help, it often will.

Deed in Lieu of Foreclosure

This is a tactic still widely used by those facing foreclosure. Because of its broad use, however, it has become a less valuable tool than it was. Nevertheless, it is something to consider.

The foreclosure process, regardless of whether your loan instrument is a mortgage or a trust deed, is time consuming and costly to the lender. Anything that can cut down on costs and time will get the lender's interest. This sometimes presents an option for you. It works like this: At the end of the foreclosure process, the lender winds up with a deed to your property. Of course, to get that deed there are attorney fees, advertising, selling the property, and so forth.

You, however, can save the lender those fees and the time spent simply by sending it a recordable deed. Consider what this means.

You are unable to make your monthly payments. You may have lost your job, or there could be illness, or whatever. The reason, here, doesn't matter. For whatever reason you can't make those payments. Three months have gone by, and the lender is threatening to file a notice of default or a complaint to start formal foreclosure action.

You realize your situation is hopeless. You simply can't come up with the money. You have already decided you're going to have to bail out of your house. But at least you want to preserve your credit.

So you contact your lender and make it this proposition: "I will execute a deed in favor of you. You will avoid having to go through the foreclosure process. You will save attorney's fees, lost interest, and time. All you have to do is to accept the deed and record it."

If the lender is likewise convinced your situation is hopeless, it may indeed be willing to accept the deed in lieu of foreclosing on your property. Remember, the foreclosure process itself can take upwards of six months. It will be losing interest on your mortgage during that period. If it can quickly take back the property and resell it, it might stand to save many thousands of dollars.

To save time and money, many, many lenders are willing to accept a deed in lieu of foreclosure. In fact, in the Southwest executing a deed in lieu of foreclosure became commonplace as that market deteriorated.

Be forewarned, however, that you should not take this step lightly. When you do so, you *lose all* of your equity. The lender doesn't pay you anything.

Further, you can only use this step, usually, once the lender is convinced you can't pay. Typically this means you will have got many months behind in your payments. If the lender thinks you can pay, it may be unwilling to accept a deed in lieu of foreclosure.

Steps to Take

If you want to avoid the foreclosure process by giving your lender a deed in lieu of foreclosure, here are the steps to take:

1. Find yourself in a predicament where you can't make your payments and you get behind in them.

2. Contact your lender and keep it closely informed of your troubles and your attempts to correct them. Typically, the lender must be convinced that your situation is hopeless before it will agree.

3. Get a commitment from the lender to accept a deed in lieu of foreclosure.

4. Have the deed made out (this can be done by a title insurance company, or sometimes the lender will prepare it), and mail it to your lender.

5. Check to see it has been properly executed (signed by the lender) and recorded.

6. Leave the property.

When a Lender Won't Accept a Deed in Lieu of Foreclosure

Sometimes the lender won't accept a deed in lieu of foreclosure. This is usually the case when the lender plans to go through judicial foreclosure.

There are usually two reasons for this. The first is that your property's value has dropped below the mortgage owed. The lender will go through judicial foreclosure and then secure a deficiency judgement against you in an attempt to recoup its losses.

Usually, however, the only time a lender will try this is if it is convinced that it can collect. If you are financially strapped and have no other assets, it would make little sense for the lender to go through judicial foreclosure (unless the instrument were a mortgage and it had no choice).

The second reason a lender will go through the whole process is because you have failed to establish communications. If, early on in your troubles, you fail to contact the lender and get to know the people in the delinquent loan department, they aren't going to be very receptive to later offers.

On the other hand, if you've contacted the lender at least once a week, shown that you've conscientiously tried to make the payments, and have had hardships that prevent this from happening, they will tend to see you as a person and not as dollar signs. In this case they are much more likely to go along with you.

Recording It Anyway

It isn't always necessary for the lender to accept the deed. In some states, in order to record a deed, both parties to it, the grantor (person giving it) and the grantee (person receiving it), have to sign and have their signatures notarized.

In a few states, however, only the grantor's signature need be notarized. If that's the case in your state, you can have the deed made out, sign it, have it notarized, and record it. In one fell swoop the property has been transferred. And the lender has no say in the matter!

You need to check with a good real estate attorney in your state to see if this applies to you. You'll also need to determine what kind of deed is appropriate (grant deed, warranty deed, quit-claim deed, etc.) and how the title should be made out so it converts correctly to the lender.

This process, however, may not preclude the lender from going forward with judicial foreclosure, if it so chooses, in order to secure a deficiency judgement against you.

Problems with Recording a Deed in Lieu of Foreclosure

The whole point of recording a deed in lieu of foreclosure is to save your credit rating. Later on when you are asked, "Have you ever lost a property through foreclosure?" you can truthfully answer that you have not.

Additionally, though the mortgage lender may report to a credit agency that you were behind in several months' payments, it may not report that you lost the property through foreclosure.

In short, your hope in recording a deed in lieu of foreclosure is that you will preserve enough of your credit that in the future you'll be able to secure another mortgage and buy another home.

It's a good hope. However, due to the widespread usage of deeds in lieu of foreclosure to avoid bad credit, lenders have become sensitive to them. Today most modern mortgage applications include two lines which read something like this:

1. Have you ever lost a property through foreclosure?
2. Have you ever given a deed in lieu of foreclosure?

Today, lenders want to know if you've ever used the deed in lieu procedure to attempt to protect your credit. If you answer yes on their form, many consider this an automatic reason to deny you a mortgage.

On the other hand, if you lie about it and the lender finds out (some lenders are notifying credit agencies about accepting deeds in lieu), it is likewise grounds for denying the mortgage, and could be considered attempted fraud.

My suggestion here is that if asked the question, you answer truthfully. But, you also include a detailed letter explaining your circumstances and why you executed the deed in lieu. Be careful to explain why your current situation is different now.

Everyone can have hard times, and lenders realize this. If you can convince them that your financial fortunes have turned around, and if you are honest and above board about it, they may take a chance on you. At least, to my way of thinking, it's a better shot than trying to sneak by and risk getting caught.

When You Have a Second Mortgage or Trust Deed

We've been assuming right along that the foreclosure process you are involved with has to do with a first mortgage. However, in many cases it's not the first, but the second or inferior mortgage that is the one which is threatening to foreclose. If this is the case, you may have additional options.

The Order of Mortgages

Before going on, let's be sure we understand how mortgages (using the term generically to include trust deeds) work when there's more than one on the property. Perhaps an example will help.

Sally and Peter bought a home three years ago. The purchase price was $200,000. They were able to secure a new first mortgage for 80 percent of the value, or $160,000. However, they didn't have the necessary $40,000 cash down payment. So the seller agreed to give them a second mortgage for $20,000. Here's how the purchase looked.

Purchase with Second Mortgage

First mortgage	$ 160,000
Second mortgage	20,000
Cash down	20,000
Purchase price	200,000

The problem is that a short time later, prices plummeted, and Sally lost her job. They couldn't afford to make the payments. Now their house was only worth $180,000, and the original seller foreclosed on the second mortgage.

To understand why the holder of the second mortgage is foreclosing, it's necessary to understand the order of mortgages. Basically, the lower the number of the mortgage, the greater its precedence. It really all has to do with when the mortgage was recorded.

A first mortgage is recorded first. A second mortgage is recorded after there is already a first on the property. In other words, it is recorded second. A third mortgage is recorded after there are already a first and a second on the property. It is recorded third. And so forth.

The mortgages need not say they are "first" or "third." In fact, there is good reason for the lender not to specify, since if a lower mortgage pays off, the higher mortgage may take its place. What gives them their position is their order of being recorded.

What's important about the order in which mortgages are recorded has to do with foreclosure. When a property goes into foreclosure and is sold at public auction "on the courthouse steps," whatever money is received goes first to pay off the first mortgage. Then, if there's anything left, the second is paid off. Finally, if there's still money left, third and higher mortgages are paid off.

It is for this reason that most institutional lenders such as banks and savings and loan associations will only lend on a first mortgage. (The exception, of course, is a home equity loan, where they will accept a secondary position.)

Thus, when Sally and Peter stopped making payments, they stopped paying on both their mortgages, the first and the second. But the holder of the second (the original seller) realized that if the first mortgage foreclosed, he could lose all his interest.

Therefore, he began making payments on the first, added that to the second, and put the second into foreclosure. (The second mortgage must provide for this process, but most do.) By foreclosing on the second, he hoped to take back the property and then resell it, thus preserving most of his $20,000.

Advantages to You When the Second Forecloses

There may be distinct advantages to you when the second forecloses. The reason is that typically the holder of the second may be the original seller or some other private individual. It may be far easier to negotiate with this person than with an institutional lender.

For example, you can contact the holder of the second mortgage and point out that you are having some difficulties. But, you hope that those problems will be shortlived. You can then make the second holder a variety of propositions, any one of which might fit your situation.

Proposals to the Holder of the Second

1. You (the holder of the second) make the payments on the first and second mortgages for six months, until I can get back on my feet. You add the amount of these payments to the second. Then, once I get back on my feet, I'll continue making payments on both mortgages. If, after six months, I'm still not financially sound, I'll execute a deed in lieu of foreclosure to you. Thus, you won't have lost much time, it will save you some money, you'll end up with a bigger second, and you won't have to take the house back. (I, on the other hand, may be able to stave off foreclosure.)

2. I'll give you a new third mortgage if you advance me the money to make payments for six months. This new third will be a balloon mortgage all due and payable in three years. You won't have to worry about foreclosing now. I hope that within three years the market will turn around and I can sell for a profit, paying off all the mortgages.

3. I'll take you in as a partner. I'll give you half interest in the property if you make the payments for a year on the first mortgage. This will avoid your having to go through foreclosure, and it will allow you to profit from future appreciation once the market turns around. I, on the other hand, will have built in some time in order to get my financial act together. (See an earlier chapter on equity sharing for details on this.)

4. I will fight your foreclosure process and delay it as long as possible, perhaps for a year or more. During that time you'll have to keep making interest payments on the first to keep it out of foreclosure. This will eat up most of your equity in your second. Since prices are falling anyhow, chances are you'll end up with nothing.

On the other hand, you allow me to sell the property even if it means a loss for you of some of your money on your second. I'll come out with clean credit, and you'll come out with at least some money.

In the case of Peter and Sally, the holder of the second mortgage might be willing to accept any of these proposals. Each of them offers the second holder something. This is opposed to taking a chance on getting far less or even nothing at all if he proceeds with the foreclosure process.

A Balloon Second

There is yet another situation some people find themselves in given today's down market. They bought their home three to five years ago with a second mortgage. Thinking property values were going to go up forever, they accepted a short term "balloon" payment on the second. Now, even though they haven't lost their jobs and aren't being threatened with imminent foreclosure on their first, that balloon payment is coming due. They can't sell or refinance to pay it off (because their house has lost value), and they don't have cash to pay it off. The balloon second is now threatening them with foreclosure. Perhaps an example will help.

Kim bought her house three years ago. The price was $150,000. She got a new first mortgage for $100,000, put down $25,000 cash and got a second mortgage from the seller for the balance of $25,000. That second mortgage, however, contained a three year balloon payment.

Purchase with Balloon Second Mortgage

First mortgage	$ 100,000
Second mortgage (balloon)	25,000
Cash down	25,000
Purchase price	150,000

What the balloon payment on Kim's second means is that three years from the date it was issued, the entire $25,000 is due. During those three years, Kim made payments on interest only. She hasn't paid back a bit of that principle.

Kim's plan had been to sell within three years and move elsewhere. She would have paid off the second from the sale.

However, with prices falling, if she now sells she won't have enough equity to use as a down payment elsewhere. Thus, selling has been virtually eliminated as a possibility.

Her fall back plan was to refinance to pay off the balloon second. She had anticipated the house would be worth at least $170,000 within three years. If she didn't want to sell, she figured she could get an 80 percent loan—that would be around $132,000—more than enough to pay off that balloon and leave her some cash.

However, with a market value of $140,000, the most she can hope to get from refinancing at 80 percent is $112,000, far short of the additional money she needs to pay off the balloon.

She doesn't have $25,000 in cash to pay off the second. She can't sell. And she can't refinance to raise that amount of money. If she does nothing, however, the holder of the second mortgage will foreclose, and she could lose the property. What can she do?

How to Handle a Balloon Payment

Kim is actually in much better shape than some of the other sellers we've come across thus far. She has a number of excellent options, providing she decides to exercise them. Here are some suggestions about what she, and you, can do in this circumstance:

1. Get a "hard money" second. Kim can go to an institutional lender, such as a bank or savings and loan, and borrow some of the money. Unfortunately, these lenders typically won't lend above 80 percent of the value of the property. Nevertheless, if the house is worth $140,000 the maximum loan amount can be $112,000. If she has a $100,000 first, that leaves $12,000 she can get on a new second. That's roughly half of what she needs.

2. Borrow from an individual. Though they typically charge much higher interest rates, individuals can lend any amount and

may be willing to make her a loan of the full $25,000 on a new second mortgage. She should check with mortgage brokers and title insurance companies, as well as with advertisements in the yellow pages to find such lenders.

3. Negotiate with the current holder of the second mortgage. Kim needs to find out what the present holder of the second intends to do with the $25,000 when he receives it. If he intends to lend it out again, her problems may be solved. She can offer to extend the second for additional years. In other words, she can offer to reborrow the money.

There is a method to doing this. First, she must be sure the holder of the second does not feel she constitutes any sort of non-payment threat. To do this she should be sure she keeps her mortgage payments (first and second) current.

Second, she needs to open negotiations early. Waiting until the balloon payment is due won't work. By then the holder of the second may already have made plans for the money. She should begin talking to him six to nine months *before* the payment is due. That way her negotiating position is far stronger.

Finally, she may want to tempt the holder of the second with a little inducement. She may offer to increase the interest rate by a point or two. The holder will be making more on his money by leaving it where it is.

Throughout the negotiations, however, Kim's goal must be to extend the term of that second for as long as possible. Ideally she'll try for a five to seven year new second. However, if she can't get it, even a three year second is better than foreclosure.

4. Negotiate a part payment. Kim can get $12,000 on a new hard money second. Offer the holder of the current second $12,000 in cash plus a $13,000 third. The downside to him is that this weakens his position (from a second to a third). The up side is that it gets nearly half his cash out and still gives him a high yielding mortgage.

In situations such as this, the second holder will usually compromise, and Kim could end up with an extended mortgage of some sort.

Occasionally, however, the second holder will demand cash. In that case, Kim's options are diminished. She can sell at a loss, or borrow at higher interest rates and hope to sell later when the market turns around.

Either way, however, her situation with a balloon coming due is still far better than the person whose house is worth less than he or she owes. If you find yourself in this situation, just remember balloon payments are almost always negotiable.

Homesteading

In good times no one ever talks about homesteading. But, when the market turns bad, it seems every other seller is ready to homestead his property. Homesteading isn't really much of a protection. The protections homesteading gives to a seller of a house in a down market are largely illusory. It only seems like it will protect you. In reality, it probably won't. Nevertheless, because so many people are interested in it, it's worth a brief discussion.

The problems have to do with the homesteading laws themselves. Most states allow an individual to homestead his property. The homestead laws are archaic, dating back to the 1930s and in some case to the 1800s. They were originally enacted to prevent unscrupulous lenders from throwing people off their farms and homes. They never were intended to protect a modern home owner from foreclosure.

How Homesteading Works

The laws for homesteading vary from state to state, but in general they work like this: By recording a "Declaration of Homestead" (you can secure the form from a title insurance company or sometimes a stationery store), you give notice to the world that your house is protected from creditors up to the maximum allowed by your state.

For example, you declare a homestead on your property. Later you go out and charge $15,000 on your Visa card and don't pay.

The bank seeks to recover the $15,000 and wants to do so by putting a lien on your property and forcing its sale. Only it can't do so because you are protected up to the amount of homesteading allowed by your state.

There are several tricky parts to this. Let's say the maximum amount you are allowed to homestead is $25,000. In other words, you can protect that amount of your equity.

But, let's say that your house is worth $150,000. The creditor, in this case the bank issuing your VISA card, can still put a lien on your property and possibly force a sale. You will be entitled to receive the first $25,000 of equity realized from the sale. But the next monies realized will go to the bank. In short, the amount of homesteading allowed is usually so small that it often doesn't pay to use the technique.

Second, homesteading only works for liens, mortgages and other debts acquired *after* you homestead. A mortgage placed on the property *before* you record a declaration of homestead doesn't apply.

In other words, you buy a home with a $100,000 mortgage on it. Later, the market turns down and you lose your job. You can't make the mortgage payments, so to avoid foreclosure you record a declaration of homestead, hoping it will stop the lender.

However, because the mortgage was placed on the property *before* the homestead was declared, it has no effect on it. The mortgage lender can proceed with foreclosure just as if the homestead weren't there. The first $100,000, in this case, will go to pay off the mortgage. Of course, you will receive additional moneys received at the sale, if any.

There is even a down side to recording a declaration of homestead in that it puts lenders on notice that you may be having financial difficulty. Once recorded, you may find lenders are reluctant to advance you additional credit and may even act to reduce the credit you already have.

11

Tax Consequences of Foreclosure or Sale in a Down Market

In this chapter we are going to consider the tax consequences of disposing of your home in a down market. However, you the reader should keep in mind that what you are going to read is a general overview. This material does not constitute legal or tax advice. For legal or tax advice you should consult with a tax professional, such as your tax attorney or CPA. While the author has endeavored to make this material up-to-date as of this writing, because tax laws and the interpretation of those laws change so frequently, readers are specifically advised not to rely on material in this chapter.

Foreclosure, for most people, is the ultimate disaster. It means you've lost your home. When you leave you won't take anything with you except your personal possessions—your equity is gone, your control over the property has vaporized, and all the money you originally invested plus your monthly payments are lost.

However, when things go wrong, they usually go very wrong, and foreclosure is no exception. You could be in store for a further blow from the Internal Revenue Service when you file your next tax return. It's possible that you might owe taxes on your foreclosure!

This shocker is something very few people understand or are ready for. However, in a down market where foreclosure is a possibility, it's something you definitely should look into.

Similarly, selling for less than you paid for your home can produce some surprising tax consequences. You might find that you owe taxes on an apparent loss!

We'll begin with a discussion of foreclosure:

How the IRS Sees a Foreclosure

It's important to understand that when you lose your property to foreclosure and walk away without a cent, it doesn't mean that you received nothing, as far as the government is concerned. Rather, for tax purposes your loss is treated as a sale, and the sale price is the amount you owed on the mortgage.

This isn't really as unreasonable as it first sounds. Remember the foreclosure procedure. Regardless of whether you had a trust deed or a mortgage, your property at some point was sold "on the courthouse steps" to the highest bidder. The highest bidder, normally, is the lender. Nevertheless, there was a sale, and the lender bid the full amount of the mortgage plus back interest, penalties, and costs.

How You Could Get a Tax Gain Out of a Real Loss

It is not inconceivable, in fact it is downright likely in many cases, that the sales price as determined by the foreclosure process is higher than your tax basis in the house. As a result, you could have a taxable gain. Perhaps a few examples will help.

Example 1—*You refinanced to pay for your children's college education.*

This is a common enough scenario. Pam and Larry bought their home ten years ago for $100,000. During that time it doubled in value to $200,000.

Their original mortgage was for $80,000. However, when it came time to put their three sons through college, they found they simply couldn't afford it. So they refinanced for 80 percent of the house's then current market value, or $160,000. They pulled $80,000 in cash out of the house and used it to pay for their kid's education, a noble purpose.

Pam and Larry's Refinance

Down payment	$ 20,000
Original mortgage	80,000
Purchase price	100,000
Appreciated value	200,000
Multiplier	x .80
Refinance	160,000
Less original mortgage	-80,000
Cash pulled out of home	80,000

The trouble is that last year Larry lost his job and Pam was not working. Their payments on the mortgage were $1,500 a month plus taxes and insurance, and within six months their savings were exhausted. They decided the only alternative was to put their home up for sale.

Only by then the market had dropped. Their home was only worth about $160,000. Since their loan was not assumable, any buyer would have to get a new loan, paying points and other costs. In other words, forgetting about commissions and closing fees to the seller, a buyer would have to pay about $167,000 to buy their $160,000 home. Naturally enough, there were no takers.

Pam and Larry didn't try any of the techniques to avoid foreclosure suggested in the last chapter. Instead, they simply allowed things to take their course. After about eight months, they were forced to leave their home, losing everything.

They were courageous people, however, and moved to a different area where Larry was able to find work, and they started over.

The next spring, they went to an accountant to get their taxes calculated and received the shock of their lives. Their accountant told them their tax basis in their house had been $100,000—the amount for which they had purchased it. On the other hand, their sale price was $160,000, the amount of the foreclosure sale. The difference, or $60,000, was a taxable gain in the year they lost the home. In their tax bracket they owed about $15,000 to the federal government plus additional taxes to their state government.

Larry and Pam were aghast. How could it be? They had lost their home. How could they owe tax on a loss? The accountant went through the figures slowly.

Pam and Larry's Gain on Their Lost Home

Sales price (at foreclosure)	$ 160,000
Purchase price (basis)	100,000
Taxable gain	60,000

"But where's the money?" Pam protested. "How can we be forced to pay taxes on money we never received?"

"Oh, but you did receive it," the accountant pointed out. He reminded them of the refinance. They pulled $80,000 in cash out of the house to pay for their children's education, $60,000 more than they had originally paid for the property.

"When you got that $60,000, you didn't need to pay taxes on it because you had simply refinanced, and there's normally no tax liability on a refinance," their accountant pointed out. "However, when you sold, you converted that into a gain, which was taxable. You did receive the money. What you were able to do was to postpone the tax on it. Once you lost the property to foreclosure, however, that tax became immediately due."

Larry and Pam learned a hard lesson as they struggled to make their tax payments.

Example 2—*You rolled over a gain from a previous personal residence when you bought the current house.*

Steve and Elaine bought their first house fifteen years ago for $40,000. When they sold it five years ago, they received $200,000. Without taking into account adjustments to basis or sales price, their gain was roughly $160,000. However, they deferred payment of taxes on that gain since within two years they bought another house for $205,000. Since the purchase price of their new house was more than the sales price of their old house, they were allowed this deferral. (We'll have more to say about deferral of gain on a personal residence shortly.)

Steve and Elaine's Deferral

Sale price of old home	$ 200,000
Purchase price of old home	40,000
Taxable gain	160,000
(Gain deferred–purchase price higher than sales price)	
Purchase price of new home	205,000
Tax basis in new property	40,000

Note: The calculations above are presented in a manner that makes them easy to understand. The IRS makes its calculations in a different manner.

Needless to say, Elaine and Steve were thrilled that they were able to roll over all their gain into their new property and not have to pay any taxes. They were even more thrilled that they were not required to put that $160,000 gain into their new home. They could do anything with it!

As it turned out, they put $40,000 down and then went on a shopping spree with the rest. They bought an expensive new car and new furniture, took a cruise, and quickly went through the remaining money.

Things seemed to have worked out perfectly, until they had to sell, three years later. Recently Elaine was transferred to a new job out of state. They had to move, so they put their home up for sale.

Only it was a down market, and their home was only worth about $190,000. By the time they figured in commissions and closing costs, they would net out only about $10,000. Nevertheless, they had to move, so they sold their home.

They moved to a new state and used the $10,000 as part of a down payment on a much less expensive home, one that cost only $120,000. They thought things had worked out pretty well, until spring, when their accountant gave them their tax bite.

She told them their tax basis was $40,000 in their last home, carried forward from their first home. When they sold for $190,000 (not considering the costs of closing, which would be calculated in a real transaction), that left them with a gain of $150,000 that was fully taxable. In their tax bracket, their combined state and federal tax bite would be roughly $45,000.

Steve and Elaine couldn't talk for a moment. They owed nearly $45,000 in taxes!

Their accountant reminded them of that $160,000 in cash they received when they sold their first home. They hadn't paid any taxes on that money. But that didn't mean the taxes were forgiven. They were simply deferred until a later date: now.

"But," Elaine pointed out, "we bought a third home. Can't we just keep rolling it over?"

The accountant smiled. She told them they surely could roll all of it over, as long as the purchase price was higher than the price for which they sold their last home.

Their faces fell. Their third home cost only $120,000, and they had sold their second for $190,000. They were $70,000 off.

The accountant pointed out that this was still better than nothing. They could defer a portion of their gain, but they would still owe taxes, in their case almost $20,000. Certainly that was better, but it was hardly good.

"Isn't there anything we can do?"

The accountant thought awhile and then suggested an alternative. She pointed out that they had two years before or after the sale of their second home to replace it with another personal residence. That two year period wasn't yet up. Why not buy yet another home for around $190,000, and then roll over all the gain into it.

"But," Steve pointed out, "We just bought a home for $120,000. We've already made our move."

"Not necessarily," the accountant pointed out. She noted that the house they rolled their money into had to be their personal residence. They could rent out their $120,000 house as an investment. And they could then purchase a more expensive (fourth) house for their personal residence, and roll their gain (defer it) into that home.

Note: This requires careful planning and sound accounting. Do not attempt this until you have explored it thoroughly with your CPA, tax attorney, or other tax professional.

Both Steve and Elaine thought that sounded good—until they realized they would have to come up with a minimum $20,000 down payment plus big monthly payments to buy a bigger, more expensive home. In the end, they just couldn't manage it financially, and they paid their tax bill.

Example 3—*You sell for less than you bought.*

Lois, a single woman, bought her first home in Arizona six years ago for $80,000. She put $15,000 down and had a first mortgage of $65,000. It was a nice home and one in which she felt comfortable. She had a job as a bank officer, and the home was close to work. She was satisfied with the property.

However, within the past three years property values around her declined. Although her job was not affected, she saw her neighbors lose their jobs and then their homes. Abandoned homes popped up around her. When some of these were vandalized, she began to worry for her safety in the neighborhood. It was at this time that she decided she ought to sell.

When she called in a real estate agent, she was told the most she could hope to get for her property was around $50,000. There were some speculators who would pay that price, then rent the property out. If she wanted to get market price, she might have to wait a year or more, and even then the best she would be likely to get was $65,000.

Lois considered. If she waited, she would be stuck in a deteriorating neighborhood in a falling market. Receiving $65,000 at the end of a year wouldn't be enough—it would barely cover her mortgage let alone her costs of sale.

On the other hand, if she were to take $55,000 now, she'd have to come up with a minimum of $10,000 just to pay down the existing mortgage so she could sell! Neither alternative seemed very attractive.

So she investigated the possibility of giving the house back to the lender. Since she worked in a bank, she was able to contact the officers in charge of repossession of homes in her area directly. She negotiated with them directly and told them either they could accept a deed in lieu of foreclosure now, or she would stop making payments, it would take them months to get her out, and she'd leave the place a mess.

The bank agreed. Lois moved out and rented.

That next spring she met her accountant to do her taxes. She pointed out that she had lost her home through foreclosure. She had lost her down payment of $15,000. She had also lost her closing costs and everything else she put into the home. She wanted the accountant to write off or deduct the loss from her taxes.

Her accountant shook his head. He asked her one question, "Was the home your personal residence?"

When she answered, "Yes," he said there was nothing she could do. No deduction for loss is allowed when the loss occurs on your personal residence.

Lois was flabbergasted. "You mean I lost over $15,000 and I can't write off a penny?!"

The accountant nodded his head sadly. He pointed out that the tax laws were filled with inequities. Even if she had been allowed to write it off, she would only be able to deduct up to $3,000 a year. (Gain is fully taxable in the year received regardless of the amount. Loss is deductible only to the extent of $3,000 a year.)

Lois felt it was a sad day indeed when the real estate market fell.

Your Situation

I've tried to touch on the most common situations. Perhaps one of them parallels your own. I want to caution you, however, from making hard and fast assumptions based on this material.

There are numerous nuances to the tax law that we haven't even touched upon. Further, Congress has a habit of changing that law almost every year. In addition, the IRS and the courts are constantly reinterpreting the law. And, finally, your situation may not as closely parallel one of those noted above as you may think.

For these reasons, I strongly urge you to see your tax professional before rushing to make judgements. It may turn out that things are a lot worse for you than you think, or a lot better!

For the Future

A word is in order here about taxes and the future of real estate. The trend in Congress seems to be to avoid raising income taxes and instead get more revenue by other means. One of the other means frequently used is to reduce the deductions allowed in real estate.

In the future it is possible, though not inevitable, that the government may disallow your deduction for state property taxes and even for part or all of the interest you pay on your home. Proposals to do both these things were presented in the 1990 Congress. (If you're alarmed about this, you may want to write your congressman!)

Such a drastic change would seriously and adversely affect real estate. Property prices would surely fall from their already low levels. In short, we could see a national housing disaster with many surprising tax consequences similar to those outlined in this chapter.

12

Financing to Get Your Money Out

Anyone who has tried to sell his home for even a short period of time quickly comes to understand that the toughest thing to deal with is liquidity. Liquidity in real estate means converting equity, or ownership that appears on paper, into hard cash. As we've noted elsewhere in this book, cash is king. And in a down market, cash is very hard to come by.

Normally, you can sell your house, and in so doing convert your equity to cash. For example, your house is worth $150,000 and you owe $50,000. Forgetting costs and commission for the moment, when you sell you can expect to receive the difference, or $100,000 in cash. This is an example of liquidity.

On the other hand, in a down market, you find that you can't sell. Or that in order to sell, you must lower your price to the point where you get far less cash out of the deal. This is an example of an illiquid market.

In this chapter we're going to look into ways of making your property more liquid in a down market. We're going to consider how you can get your cash out.

Refinancing

Usually the easiest way to turn your equity, or part of it, into cash is to refinance. You don't need a buyer for this. What you need is the ability to make increased monthly payments.

Let's take the earlier example of a person who owes $50,000 with a house that's worth $150,000. This person has $100,000 in equity.

However, if he tries to sell in a down market, it's unlikely he'll be able to convert that equity to cash. On the other hand, he can get a sizeable amount of cash out in a refinance.

As a general rule of thumb, you can refinance for up to 80 percent of the market value of your home. (In some cases you may be able to refinance for as much as 90 percent of value. Check with your lender.) Further, as an owner/occupant you usually qualify for slightly better terms and a slightly lower interest rate. Here's how it would work out in our example:

Typical Refinance

Current market value	$ 150,000
Multiplier (80 percent)	x .80
Maximum mortgage value	120,000
Less existing mortgage	-50,000
Less costs of refi	-5,000
Maximum cash from refi	65,000

In our example, the seller could refinance, without selling the property, and get $65,000 out. He could then take this money and use it as a down payment on another home. And, conceivably, he could rent the old home to make the mortgage payments.

Note: If you want to refinance your old home in order to get money out for a down payment on a new home, be sure you refi at least three months before you purchase the new home. The reason is the lender on the new home won't allow you to *borrow* money for the down payment. On the other hand, if you already have borrowed the money (past tense) and have established a loan on another property for it, then, as strange as it may seem, the money to make the down payment is not considered borrowed!

Who Will Lend You Money?

In the past the primary source of refinancing money was savings and loan associations. However, with the crisis of the early 1990s, and so many S&Ls going bankrupt, the source of funds has shifted to an almost even split between S&Ls and commercial banks. Today, your bank may be able to make you a better deal on a refinance than your savings and loan. Both are worth checking out.

Ways to Refinance

There are basically two ways to refinance. One is to get a new first mortgage paying off the existing mortgage(s) on your property. The other is to keep your existing mortgage and get a new second.

Many would-be sellers faced with these alternatives really don't know how to decide. Here are some guidelines.

When You Have a Lower Interest Rate Mortgage

If your existing first mortgage is lower than the current market rate, you may be better off hanging onto it. For example, the current market rate may be 10 percent. But, your current first mortgage is for 8 percent. If you were to refinance by getting a new first, you'd be exchanging an 8 percent mortgage for a 10 percent one. That hardly makes much sense.

The refi gets tricky, however, when you consider the alternative: getting a second for the difference between the existing first and the maximum loan amount. Often the seconds are more expensive than a new first. A second may carry an interest rate of 12 percent, while a first may only be at 10 percent. Perhaps an example will help.

Refinancing with a New First
New first at 10% $ 120,000
  Effective interest rate: 10%

Refinancing with a New Second
Existing first at 8% $ 50,000
New second at 12%   70,000
  Approximate effective interest rate: 11%

In the above example, the combination of a low interest rate first with a high interest rate second produces a higher overall interest rate than simply getting a new low interest rate first.

The key here is the size of your existing first mortgage. If you have a much bigger first mortgage at a low interest rate, then you are probably going to be better off combining it with a smaller second mortgage, even at a higher interest rate, as long as the interest rate of the second isn't too high.

On the other hand, if you have a smaller first and are getting a big second, as in our example, then perhaps refinancing with a new first will make more sense. The loan officer who handles your refinance should be able to set up both alternatives for your specific case so you can see which gives you the lowest overall interest rate.

Consider Monthly Payments
The interest rate isn't everything. A big consideration for most people is the monthly payments. If you want the *lowest* possible monthly interest rates, then you should consider whether your existing first mortgage is stale.

A "stale" mortgage is one which has been on the property a long time. In the first years of the mortgage, almost all your monthly payment goes to interest, and very little goes to principal. For example, on a $100,000 loan at 12 percent for thirty years, your initial monthly payment is around $1,029. However, of that amount only about $29 goes to repaying your principal. The rest, or $1,000, goes toward interest!

However, as you pay off the loan, more and more of your payment goes toward principal. By year twenty nearly a third is going to principal. By year twenty-five, nearly half. What this means is that if you have an existing mortgage on your property that is stale, a lot of your payment is going toward principal.

There's nothing wrong with this since your equity is being built up with each payment. However, if your goal is to get lower payments, you might be willing to forego that equity buildup.

In our above example, let's say a $40,000 loan was originally $100,000 and it was taken out about twenty-five years ago. The seller is making payments of roughly $1,000 a month of which $700 is going to principal.

He now refinances for the same interest rate and term. Immediately his payments on that $40,000 are going to be cut by about a half. In other words, the payments on a $40,000 mortgage at 12 percent are only about $400 a month.

If he were to refinance for $100,000 at the same interest and term, his payments would remain the same ($1,000), only he would be able to withdraw $60,000 in cash!

In short, if you have a mortgage on your property that you took out a long time ago (usually it must be more than ten years old for any significant amount to be paid down), you may be able to refinance at close to your current payments, yet get cash out.

It's definitely something to consider.

When You Can Get a Home Equity Loan

Another consideration is the type of mortgage you get. Today many seconds are available in the form of a home equity loan.

A home equity is a special kind of loan that many lenders are offering. It may offer certain advantages, as well as disadvantages, to you when you're trying to get your equity out.

Among the biggest advantages is flexibility. Often you can take the money out only when you need it. For example, you can refinance, put the mortgage on your property, yet not receive the cash. (Of course, no interest is being charged during this period.)

When you want the cash, as for example when you decide to make a down payment on another home, you simply write a check for it. In this fashion, you don't pay interest on money until you actually need it.

Another advantage is that many banks, in particular, are promoting home equity loans at this time. As a result, they are offering greatly reduced terms. In some states, for example, the lender will offer the mortgage at no cost to you. It will pay for an appraisal on your house and waive document, recording, title search, escrow, and other costs. This is different from conventional refinancing, where the costs of the mortgage can often equal 5 percent of the amount borrowed.

A disadvantage of a home equity loan is that frequently it is only available in an adjustable rate form. This means your interest rate moves up or down depending on market conditions. (I'll have more to say about this, shortly.)

Further, the rate is often a point or two higher than regular first mortgages. For example, a regular first mortgage (adjustable) may have an annual percentage rate (APR) of 10 percent. But a home equity line of credit at the same time may carry an APR of 12 percent.

In short, you may pay more interest for the home equity line of credit (second mortgage) than for a comparable first mortgage.

One additional comment about home equity lines of credit is that new federal regulations took effect in 1989 requiring much more disclosure about these loans than in the past. Previously some borrowers were not aware the loan involved a second mortgage on the property, nor did they realize they could lose their homes if they did not make their payments. Today the disclosure rules are quite extensive and have worked to reduce abuse.

When You Can Get a Low Interest Rate Second

Some lenders are offering low interest rate second mortgages. These should not be confused with home equity loans.

These low interest rate seconds often carry a rate that is virtually equal to a first. For example, a first may offer an interest rate of 10 percent while a low interest rate second may have a rate of only 10.5 percent.

Usually S&Ls offer these low rate seconds. But typically they do not promote them. You have to ask if you're going to find one.

Also, the lenders typically do not offer any special deals on costs. You end up paying for points, title insurance, escrow, appraisal, and other fees. As noted earlier, this can amount to upwards of 5 percent of the loan amount (more on smaller loans).

Variable vs. Fixed Interest Rate Mortgage

There are numerous kinds and types of mortgages available today. But almost all of them are of two basic varieties: the fixed, where the interest rate does not vary for the life of the mortgage; and the variable, where the interest rate moves up and down depending on external factors (such as the cost of money to the lender).

While a detailed discussion of the differences between these two types of loans is beyond the scope of this book, we should look at the pros and cons each offers when you want to refinance because you can't sell. (For more information, check into *Making Mortgages Work For You,* McGraw-Hill, 1987, by my favorite author.)

Fixed Rate

A fixed rate mortgage offers you peace of mind. You know what your interest rate is and, consequently, what your monthly payments will be. You don't have to worry that next month you'll be paying a hundred dollars more for the mortgage than this month.

The drawback to this type of mortgage, however, is that the interest you pay is often higher, initially, than that for a variable rate mortgage. This can be a distinct disadvantage if you only plan to keep the house a short time, until the market turns around.

Variable Rate

Here, as mentioned, the interest rate and hence the monthly payment will vary. Often there are caps or limits on the amount the interest rate or monthly payment can rise in any given time period. But even so, they can go up. (They can also go down if the cost of money drops, but I've never heard anyone complain about this!)

These variable rate mortgages (also called "adjustable") also may offer you a big advantage, if you're only refinancing as an interim measure. They can give you initially lower payments.

Most variables offer a teaser or introductory rate. This is an interest rate that is lower than the current market rate for mortgages, sometimes as much as 4 or 5 percent lower. The idea is that most people really don't want the worry of fluctuating payments; hence they won't normally take out these loans. However, they can be induced to take them out if the initial interest rate, and thus initial monthly payments, are lower.

Consider, on a conventional loan of $100,000 at 10 percent, the monthly payment is around $875. At the same time, however, a variable rate mortgage with a teaser of 7 percent will start you off with monthly payments of about $600 a month.

That's a savings of about $275 a month between the two mortgages. Is it any wonder that variables amount to around half of all mortgages at any given time?

The problem, of course, is that the teaser rate doesn't last. Often it will disappear after six months. Sometimes, depending on the mortgage, the interest rate you pay may gradually rise over several years until it is at market rate. (Of one thing you can be sure, eventually the variable rate will rise until it matches the market rate.)

This teaser, however, can offer an advantage to you, if you are refinancing because you can't sell. Presumably, you anticipate being able to sell someday, you hope within a couple of years. When you do sell, you plan to pay off the variable rate mortgage you take out when you refinance.

Therefore, why not get a variable with lower initial payments? You'll be making lower payments while you own the property, and just about the time (you hope) the payments get really high, you'll be able to sell and get rid of the mortgage.

Many sellers are doing just that. However, keep in mind there is a catch. If housing prices don't improve, and if you aren't able to resell, in a few years you'll be paying market interest rates on that variable. (In some cases the variable is set so that you end up paying above market rates.)

Refinancing before the Market Drops

There is one additional problem with refinancing in a down market that we haven't considered: namely, the falling market can adversely affect your ability to refinance.

In our first example, we considered someone whose house was worth $150,000. Because he could typically borrow 80 percent of value, he could refinance for approximately $120,000.

However, what if he hesitates and waits six months. Perhaps during those six months his house will drop $15,000 in value, to only $135,000. Now, since he can only borrow 80 percent, his maximum loan amount becomes $108,000. He's lost the ability to borrow $12,000 on the property.

Loss in Refinancing Value Due to Falling Market

Market value	$ 150,000
80% Refinance	120,000
Six months later:	
Market value	135,000
80% Refinance	108,000

The rule here is that in a falling market, you want to refinance as soon as possible to get the maximum amount of cash out of your home. The longer you wait, the less you may be able to borrow.

A good alternative is the equity line of credit discussed earlier. Here you can place a second mortgage on your property for a set amount of money, yet not actually receive that money (or pay interest on it) until later. This way you can have your cake, and eat it, too!

Seller's Seconds

Another way of refinancing that is coming back into vogue is to refinance the buyer, instead of yourself, the seller. In other words, you lend the buyer the money to purchase your home. This is usually in the form of a second mortgage, but, if your house is free and clear, or if you have a small first that the buyer can pay off, it can be in the form of a new first mortgage.

There are certain plusses to you for making the buyer a loan. The biggest is that it may allow you to make a sale that you would otherwise not be able to make.

For example, you're selling a home for $150,000 and you owe $100,000, but there are no takers. So you advertise (or instruct your agent to advertise) that you'll give the buyer a second mortgage at 8 percent, when the current interest rate is 10 percent. Further, you'll only require 10 percent down.

What you accomplish when you do this is to open the market up to many more potential buyers. Many buyers won't be able to qualify for an institutional loan. Others won't have the traditional 20 percent down.

In short, you may be able to sell for a higher price or sooner, if you can offer to refinance the property yourself.

Cashing in a Second

It may be possible to get cash for the second you give a buyer of your home. There are investors who will buy your second for cash. Be aware, however, that you will have to discount it.

"Discounting" means you sell the second for less than its face value. You might have a second of $10,000 which you sell for cash for $7,000. The $3,000 difference is the discount.

Seconds are discounted to raise their yield. Perhaps you gave the buyer a below-market interest rate. However, in order to sell the second, you must offer someone a higher than market interest rate. You do this by discounting the mortgage.

Again, check with a mortgage broker to figure out the exact amount of discount you will need to charge. Keep in mind, however, that the higher the interest rate and the shorter the term, the easier it is to sell a second.

Drawbacks to Seller Refinancing

Of course, this isn't a panacea. When you carry the paper, generally speaking you get a less qualified buyer. That means there is a greater chance the buyer will not be able to make the payments and you might need to take the property back—a complex, lengthy, and costly process (see chapter ten on foreclosure).

Further, there are some unscrupulous buyers out there who will try to get in with no down payment. They may then live in the property for a period of time, or rent it out, and not make any payments to you! Their whole goal may be to strip the income from your home while delaying foreclosure as long as possible. In so doing they may collect upwards of a year's income.

You, on the other hand, would have to foreclose, in the meantime losing the money you hoped to get on your second mortgage as well as having to make payments on your first.

IRS Complications

There may also be tax consequences when you carry the paper on your home sale. You should always consult with a tax professional such as a CPA or a tax attorney before the sale to make sure you understand those consequences.

There could be one last drawback to lending money to a buyer at *below market interest rates*. Sometimes the IRS will look askance at this. It will say, in effect, that by lowering the interest rate on the mortgage you give to your buyer, you were enabled to receive a higher price. Thus, indirectly, you're still getting the market interest rate. (No one ever said the IRS didn't have convoluted thinking!)

As a result, for tax purposes the IRS may impute interest to your loan. This means it may calculate the interest you receive at full market value, even though the mortgage you gave the buyer is for less.

In other words, you may have given your buyer an 8 percent mortgage rate. However, at the time the market rate for mortgages may be 10 percent. You will receive payments based on 8 percent, which naturally, you will have to declare as income for tax purposes. However, the IRS may impute the interest to 10 percent. In short, you could end up paying taxes on 10 percent even though you only actually received 8 percent!

Of course, it might be worth it, *if* the lower interest rate allowed you to sell your home. Again, check with your tax professional.

13

Beware of Sales
Exhaustion

There is an old Chinese tale of a man, Chou, whose job it was to build a great ship for the emperor. Chou had been appointed to the job because of his family's position in the empire, even though he didn't know the first thing about ship building. Chou did understand, however, that if he succeeded in building a great ship according to the emperor's plans, he would prosper for the rest of his life, so his enthusiasm was unbounded.

Chou went to the wharf and hired the best shipbuilder he could find. But the shipbuilder soon told him the emperor's plans made no sense and the ship couldn't be built. So Chou hired another shipbuilder and when that person couldn't do the work, he hired yet another.

The third shipbuilder said he would try, and work began. But soon the workmen laid down their tools, saying the wood that was locally available could not be carved to fit the plans. The shipbuilder said it was hopeless.

Chou was in despair. But he pulled himself together and travelled to a distant forest, where he hired men to cut trees and then hired others to cart them back. Once again work progressed.

Soon the ship was nearly built. Then a workman tipped over a fire pot used for heating pitch (which was used to seal the planks), and the entire ship was burned to the ground. Chou was depressed for days. "Why are these things happening to me?" he asked. Eventually he pulled himself together and told the shipbuilder to start over.

Once again the ship was almost built when the shipbuilder came to Chou and said that he had just discovered the wood had worms in it. It would never sail. As soon as a strong wind caught the sails, the mast would collapse and the keel would crack.

At this last report, Chou threw up his hands in despair. He walked away from the nearly completed ship. He stopped the first man he met and asked him, "Would you like to gain the emperor's favor and prosper for the rest of your life? All you have to do is finish that ship."

The man was astonished. "But, why don't you finish it and present it to the Emperor yourself?"

"Don't ask," Chou said. The man looked at the ship, which merely needed a little painting to be done, and agreed.

The new man finished the ship and told the Emperor it was ready. On a grand day the Emperor came to the port to watch the ship being launched, proclaimed it a great ship, and gave the new man immense wealth. Then the emperor left and never came back to the ship again.

The moral to this story is that Chou, and a great many people the world over, often give up out of mental exhaustion just before reaching their goal. It wasn't simply the wormy wood that did Chou in; it was the cumulative effect of all the difficulties he encountered along the way. The wormy wood was just the last straw. It was what made the task seem hopeless.

However, to someone coming in fresh, that last problem was trivial. The new man realized the emperor probably would never sail in the boat anyway; he just wanted to see something he had decreed done. So he did it and took the credit and the rewards.

What Is Real Estate Sales Exhaustion?

Much the same thing happens when you try to sell your home in a down market. Cathy and Ed had to move because of a job change, and put their $300,000 home in the San Francisco Bay Area up for sale. They anticipated they would get their price in a reasonable amount of time. They paid someone to come in and completely repaint it, and they replaced worn carpeting with brand new carpets. They were confident and enthusiastic.

But time went by and there were few prospective buyers who came to look at the home. Their agent called infrequently only to report how bad the market was.

After a couple of months Ed and Cathy decided that to get a buyer they would have to lower their price. So they dropped it down to $289,000, even though they knew that six months earlier houses similar to theirs, though in worse shape, had sold for over $300,000.

Still nothing happened. Still there were no offers.

They switched agents and were told that perhaps new landscaping would help. So they hired a landscape designer to come in, and at great expense planted new lawns and shrubs. The place did indeed look wonderful. And soon they got an offer. It was for $250,000, $39,000 less than they were asking.

"Ridiculous," they said and countered at $285,000. The would-be buyer simply walked away. And their house sat and sat.

By now things were getting financially tough. Ed was living in a distant city where his new job was located, and Cathy was staying in the house. Living apart was taking its toll on them. So they decided on a big price drop. They lowered their price to $269,000, a $20,000 drop. They reasoned that it was a big loss, but at least they'd be done with the house.

Only there were no buyers. They called the agent who had originally brought in the $250,000 offer, but he said his buyers had already purchased elsewhere.

Finally, after several months, someone offered $230,000. Ed and Cathy didn't argue. They took it.

Despair

Real estate sales exhaustion is a combination of despair and fatigue. It's effect is cumulative. Usually there's no one incident that causes it, although the last misfortune to befall usually is the one that causes you to say, "Get me out at any price!"

My feeling is that the real problem is one of desperation. In a down market with things seemingly going from bad to worse, it's easy to forget that any house can be sold. After awhile we begin to think ours will never make it; that our property will be the one that goes all the way to zero in value.

Our situation is often made even more urgent because of financial pressures. We simply may not have enough money to make the payments. Or, we may be forced to move away because of a job change or other reason.

Keeping a Positive Outlook

If you have problems financially, if your house isn't selling as soon or for as much as you hope, it's definitely depressing. As to practical suggestions, you will want to go back and reread many of the previous chapters in this book which can give you helpful clues on getting that property sold.

However, it's equally important that you be aware of seller exhaustion. There will be many times when you feel like throwing up your hands and saying, "Out, at any price!"

You must be aware that you aren't the only one to experience this feeling. You must also be aware that it's a psychological trap.

Don't Be a Highly Motivated Seller

Many savvy buyers are looking for sellers who are having real estate exhaustion. Many books and articles are written advising buyers to seek out these "highly motivated" sellers.

The idea is that when a seller gets exhausted from the process of selling, he will accept any kind of low-ball offer, even one that is far below the true value of his property.

In our earlier example, Ed and Cathy might very well have sold their house for tens of thousands of dollars more, if they had tried some of the techniques mentioned in this book. But, because of sales exhaustion, they gave up. Once the exhaustion set in, they took the first low-ball offer that came along.

You want buyers to realize you are a motivated seller, that you are anxious to dispose of your property. However, you don't want them to realize you are *highly* motivated. It's a fine line, but the difference is important. In the first case you will negotiate. In the second, like Chou in our first example, you'll give away your fortunes.

How to Avoid Sales Exhaustion

You've already taken the first step. Simply being aware that it exists will help. When things look darkest, when you just want to wash your hands of the property, when you feel you can't stand attempting to sell it for another instant, that's the time to stand back and ask yourself this question: "Am I experiencing real estate sales exhaustion?"

Just knowing it's not necessarily your circumstances, but a psychological effect, can be quite helpful.

Do Positive Things

If you think you may be experiencing real estate sales exhaustion, it's time to do positive things, relative to real estate.

You can read books such as this and see if you've followed through on all the suggestions. Maybe there are many things you can do that you haven't considered. What about renting out the house? What about promotions? What about some cleaning and painting that you never got around to doing? What about some additional advertising?

Call up your agent, if you have one, and see about getting together for a brainstorming session. But beware of an agent who tries to put down your house or overemphasizes the bad market.

He or she may simply be trying to get you into real estate sales exhaustion so you'll throw away your property and they can collect an easy commission. If your agent isn't supportive, it's definitely time to get a better agent. (See my book, *Tips And Traps When Selling Your Home,* McGraw-Hill, 1990, for clues on getting rid of a bad agent.)

Talk to property management people. Sometimes they have ideas new to you on how to rent your property for a profit. Sometimes in properties they manage they convert tenants to buyers and, over a period of time, may actually be able to sell your home for you!

Don't Give Up

The most important thing is to get out of that feeling of hopelessness. Keep in mind that any house can be sold in any market. Also remember the present down market isn't going to last forever. Just a couple of years ago your very house was probably soaring in value with prices appreciating monthly. That could happen again in the not too distant future. If you simply hang on long enough, you probably will come out a winner.

Yes, you may have to sell for less than you want. Yes, you may have to give onerous terms (for you) to the buyer in order to get that sale. But always be sure that no matter what price you sell for, no matter what terms you give, you're doing it because it's the smart thing to do at the time. Don't be like Chou and his boat. Don't give away a fortune to the first man who comes by. A good sale may be just around the corner.

14

When the Next Upturn Comes

A new myth about real estate is gaining credence. It is that real estate will continue to fall rapidly or to decline gradually for a long period of time, perhaps ten or fifteen years. Some are even talking of losing 2 to 5 percent per year on the value of homes almost indefinitely. Just as a short time ago the perception was that real estate could only go up, now it seems to be that it can only go down.

Don't believe it. Real estate will not continue down, just as it didn't continue up.

One day down the road, in, we hope, the not too distant future, buyers are going to wake up to discover there's a housing shortage, houses are affordable, and they'd best get one soon while they're still available.

Sellers will also wake up and see more buyers coming into the market and will, tentatively at first, begin raising their prices. Very soon everyone will begin to realize the worst is past, and before you know it, the next real estate boom will be upon us.

In the midst of the current doom and gloom over a real estate recession, it's important to keep one's perspective and remember that the residential real estate market, like every other market in the world, is cyclical. It has its ups, and it has its downs. And as night follows day and day follows night, the real estate market will move up and down and up again.

All of which is to say, keep a positive attitude. Things will surely get better. If you can hang onto your property, do so. Some day, before long, you will be able to sell it for a surprisingly large amount of money!

Index

Advertising:
   billboard and poster, 41-43, 51
   cable television, 41, 51
   local paper, 38, 51
   paying for, 39-40
   real estate broker and, 30-32
   selling by owner and, 45
   sign, "For Sale," 41-43, 44-45
   splitting the cost of, 39
Agent, real estate. See Real estate broker
Appraisal, free, 23
Appraiser, independent, 25
Auctions, home:
   auction companies, 60
   auctioneer, 48, 49, 52-53, 57, 58-59
   builders', 48
   buyers, attracting, 50-51
   combination, 55-59
   documents for, 58, 59
   examination period, 51-52
   individual, 48
   "Leaving Town Auction," 49-55
   of listed houses, 55
   real estate broker's role in, 50, 55, 56, 59
   and reserve price, 54-55, 57-58, 59
   terms of sale, 53-54

Baby boomers, 2-3
Bailing out:
   the decision, 127-30
   equity consideration, 126, 130, 132, 133-34
   moving, 135-36
   timing, 131-33
   in "upside down" position, 135
Balloon second mortgage, 158-61
Bargain prices, 8, 14, 77-78, 92, 116
Broker, real estate. See Real estate broker
Builders:
   in a down market, 100-102
   and promotional giveaways, 72
   trading houses with, 102-109
Buyer:
   appeal, 92-93
   fantasies of, 71
   imagination of, 62
   motivation of, 77-80
Buyer's market, 8
Buy low and sell low, 7-11

Capital gain, 11, 106, 122, 164-69, 171
Caravaners, 35-36
Cleaning and painting. See Improvements

Commission, broker:
 fixed fee, 89-90
 low, 86-91
 saving, 93-94, 98
 setting, 88
 splitting, 32-35
 typical, 29
Contingency offer, 8, 10
Credit rating, 139-40, 151, 154
"Curb appeal," 66

Deed in lieu of foreclosure, 150-
 54
Default, 142-43

Equity:
 calculating, 130
 cashing in, 173, 174
 losing all, 151
 transferring, 9, 10
Exclusive Right to Sell listing,
 40, 86-87
Exposure for your house:
 caravaners, 35-36
 in a down market, 29
 importance of, 27-28
 paying for, 33-43
 phone services, 46
 real estate board presentations,
  36-38
 real estate broker and, 29-33,
  46
 selling by owner and, 43-45,
  46
 splitting the cost, 33-34

"Fixer-upper," 61
Foreclosure:
 avoiding, 149-54
 credit rating and, 139-40
 deed in lieu of, 150-54

default and, 140-41, 142-43
deficiency judgement, 148-49
equity of redemption after,
 145, 148
judicial process, 146-48
on mortgage, 140-41, 146-48
redemption period, 143-144,
 148
sale to highest bidder, 139,
 144-45
on second mortgage, 155-58
tax consequences of, 163-71
on trust deed, 141-45
For Sale By Owner (FSBO). See
 Selling by owner
"For Sale" signs:
 auction, 56
 broker, 41-43
 open house, 42
 by owner, 44-45, 92

Home equity loan, 177-78
Homesteading, 161-62

Improvements:
 clean and paint, 62, 63, 68
 checking on comparables, 24
 "curb appeal," 66
 "fixer-upper," 61
 ideas, architect's, 66-67
 ideas, interior designer's, 65-
  66
 spending enough, 64, 68
 spending too much, 62-63, 68

Lease option, 109-114
Low commission agent, 86-91

Marketing your house, 16, 17
Market value, determining, 17,
 18, 20, 21-26

Median priced homes, 4, 24
Mortgage:
  first, 175-76
  fixed, 179-80
  foreclosure on, 146-48
  losing, 144
  non-assumable, 107, 108
  second, 175-76, 179
  variable, (adjustable) 178,
    179, 180-81
Multiple Listing Service (MLS):
  comparable sales source, 23
  exposure of your house, 31,
    43,
  with low commission agent,
    86, 87, 88, 89, 91

National Association of Realtors,
  4, 101

"On the court house steps" sale,
  139, 145, 147, 156
Overbuilding, 4-5

Packaging, 115-17
Paper profit, 20
Partnership, 117-23
Positive thinking, 34, 188
Price:
  bargain, 8, 14
  of comparable sales, 18, 22-24
  determining, 16, 21-26
  reality vs. fantasy, 18
  reduction, 7-8, 8-11
  today's, 20-21
  yesterday's, 18-20, 21
  See also Market value,
    determining
Promotional giveaways:
  by builders, 72
  buyer motivation, 71, 77-80

cost, 72-77
drawbacks, 81-82
list of, 83

Real estate, commercial, 6
Real estate attorney, services for:
  auction sales, 54, 58, 59
  contingency clauses, 10
  deficiency judgements, 148-
    49
  foreclosures, 144, 145, 147,
    149, 153
  partnership documents, 121-
    22
  sales agreements, 45
  selling by owner, 45, 95
  time-sharing, 123-24
Real estate broker:
  advertising, 30-31
  and auctions, 50, 55, 56, 59
  comparable sales source, 23
  expenses of, 30, 31, 32-33
  median sales price source, 23
  motivating, 37
  as publicist, 28, 29
  See also Commissions, broker
Real estate bubble, 6
Real estate taxes, 6, 171. See also
  Tax considerations
Real estate values:
  falling, 1-6
  future of, 191-92
  paper profit, 20
  relative, 13-14
  yesterday's, 21
Recession, 1-6, 100-109
Refinancing:
  cashing in equity, 173, 174
  home equity loan, 177-78
  in a down market, 181-82
  lease option and, 114

for liquidity, 173
mortgage, new first, 175-76
mortgage, new second, 175-76
mortgage, stale, 176-77
seller's seconds, 182-83
sources, 175
Renting:
    with lease option, 109-114
    trade up and, 103
Reserve price, 54-55, 57-58, 59

Sale of comparables:
    quality check of, 23-24
    median price for, 23-24
    sources for finding, 22-23
    time element in, 17, 18
Sales exhaustion, 185-90
Second mortgage (or trust deed), 155-61
Seller, highly-motivated, 37, 188
Selling by owner:
    broker, alternating with, 46
    buyer appeal, 92-93

disadvantages of, 94-95
exposure of your home, 43-46
low commission agent and, 91
price flexibility, 93
saving on commission, 93-94, 98
timing, 86
Sell low and buy low, 7-11

Tax considerations of:
    foreclosures, 163-71
    partnerships, 122
    price reduction, 11
    seller refinancing, 183-84
    trade ups, 105-106
Taxes, real estate. See Real estate taxes
Time-sharing, 123-24
Title transfers, 22
Trade up:
    advantages, 99-105
    pitfalls, 105-109
Trust deed foreclosure, 142-45